The Life Coaching Handbook

Everything You Need To Be An Effective Life Coach

Curly Martin

Crown House Publishing Limited
www.crownhouse.co.uk
www.crownhousepublishing.com

First published by
Crown House Publishing Ltd
Crown Buildings, Bancyfelin, Carmarthen, Wales, SA33 5ND, UK
www.crownhouse.co.uk

and

Crown House Publishing Company LLC
6 Trowbridge Drive, Suite 5, Bethel, CT 06801, USA
www.crownhousepublishing.com

First published 2001.
Reprinted 2002 (twice), 2003 (twice), 2004 (three times), 2005,
2006 (twice). 2007, 2009, 2011, 2012, 2015.

British Library Cataloguing-in-Publication Data
A catalogue entry for this book is available
from the British Library.

Print ISBN 978-189983671-0
Mobi ISBN 978-184590214-8
ePub ISBN 978-184590334-3

LCCN 2003101914

Printed and bound in the UK by
Bell & Bain Ltd., Thornliebank, Glasgow

Accl___ book

"A first class manual, and a must for every aspiring coach.
Absolutely terrific!"
– *Fiona Harrold,* author of *Be Your Own Life Coach.*

"

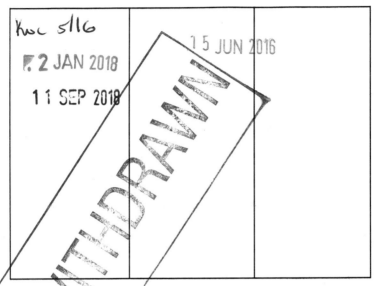
ed

or

to
time

er

l
e
nd
er
well
ial
the

.

ed

– *Georg Guy,* Cabin Services Manager and Airline Trainer of
Pilots and Cabin Crew.

**To my husband Pete,
my mother and my sisters with love**

Author's Note

Since writing this book in 2000/2001 the life coaching profession has moved from obscurity into the light of the public domain in Europe. Life coaching is frequently in the media, with life coaches enthusiastically producing press releases, presenting reality television shows, and radio programmes all actively raising the awareness of our amazing profession. Blue chip companies and small businesses alike, after hiring life coaches to improve the work/life balance of their employees and reduce work-related stress, have also discovered an increase in performance, motivation and results.

To support my readers, I now offer an accredited life coach training course based upon the principles within this book. You will watch demonstrations and practice the coaching models described here. When you qualify, you join an elite group of achievers and you will be able to declare to your clients that you have trained with a pioneer of life coaching. You can find details of the life coaching diploma course on page 201.

Life coaching is an exceptionally rewarding, passionate, exciting, challenging and enlightening profession and I consider myself blessed and honoured to be part of this life-changing revolution. Join us and make the world a better place, starting with your first client.

Curly Martin
June 2005

Table of Contents

Acknowledgments

I would like to thank all my coaches, for reminding me of what I was achieving, even when I felt I was standing still, and to all the Neuro-Linguistic Programming trainers who have influenced me – with special thanks to Dave Marshall, Roger and Louise Terry, and Katrina Patterson.

I am grateful for Steve Creffield's guidance and training on the benefits of understanding Spiral Dynamics, and for the patience my friends demonstrated in understanding the times when I couldn't "come out to play." Thanks to my family and relatives who supported me though the cancer treatment and encouraged me to write.

Thanks also to my friend and literary adviser, Colin Edwards, for his wizardry, which provided the means for my work to get to the publishers, and his wife Mary for allowing me to call at any time of day, and any day of the week.

To Ann Williams, a very special thanks, for teaching me how to drain the build-up of lymph from my right arm with a special massage technique which I practise every day. Her love and expertise gave me back the use of my arm and my ability to type.

I am ever indebted to Dr Faisal Samji, who saved my life and even became my bridesmaid.

Last, but far from least, I thank my husband, Peter, who allowed me to shout at him when I felt overwhelmed and for "being there" for me during the bleak times. His love and thoughtfulness gave me the space and time to write.

Introduction

'Life coaching is about transformation –
from a caterpillar into a butterfly'

Life coaching is about gap analysis that closes the gap between life and dreams.

Life coaching can be compared to motorway maintenance and construction. It fills and removes the ruts of life to build a smooth surface. Then life's journey takes the traveller to the destinations that they really want to visit, rather than remain in the slow lane of inactivity, drifting without purpose or direction.

If you want to make a difference in your life and the lives of others, become a life coach. This is a profession that brings joy to the client and the coach, and this handbook shows you how you can achieve these amazing rewards.

If you are considering life coaching as a career, this book will be your coach. It reveals how coaching works, how to start and grow your own practice and how to market your services.

If you are already a life coach, this book is your reference guide and reminder of how to build and develop your practice.

The book is in two parts. The first, **The Coaching Process**, covers the fundamentals of life coaching, the important differences between coaching on the one hand and counselling and therapy on the other. It describes the essential basic skills of great communication that are crucial to your success.

You will discover a step-by-step model to help you turn enquiries into paying clients, who are the lifeblood of any practice. The model is designed to help you to talk about your profession in an interesting way to create enthusiasm and desire. There are ideas on one-line conversation openers to help you hook the interest of every casual enquirer.

You are guided through a life coaching session and offered an approach to use during the first coaching call. This ensures that you fully understand your clients' aims and goals and it can be used to help clients identify their individual goals. Use it to make your life coaching process easy and effective.

The second part, **Advanced Life Coaching Skills**, identifies selected Neuro-Linguistic Programming techniques that are particularly valuable within the coaching context. State control, for both you and your clients, is described so that you coach from a peak state that you can access whenever you need it.

Rapport-building skills are extensively covered through representational systems (Chapter Eleven), Milton language (Chapter Thirteen), Meta-language (Chapter Fourteen), Meta-programs (Chapter Fifteen) and metaphors for life coaching (Chapter Sixteen). Chapter Seventeen (Spiral Coaching) covers thinking patterns and how to identify and use them to best coaching advantage. Within the second part of the book there are also different methods that you will use with each different client, and each of the methods described works independently of the others. When developing your practice, you need to be flexible and have the ability to select the model or method best suited for each client–coach relationship. For one client you may decide to concentrate on the Spiral Coaching model's thinking patterns. You may need to develop your relationship with a new client and concentrate on utilising the benefits of representational systems, whereas if you need leverage to motivate a client you could identify his or her Meta-programs. Interestingly, during a coaching programme with a client, you may employ all the different methods portrayed.

Chapter Eighteen contains practical advice drawn from long experience of actually operating a successful practice. This is where you find the "trade secrets" and some valuable marketing information.

The final chapter looks at specialisations within the profession. It identifies the main categories of specialisation and describes how you can use skills from other professions and industries within your life coaching practice.

Use this book as a guide for creating and sustaining your practice. Use it to learn or enhance your skills for working with clients. Use it to start a small, part-time practice that you can gradually develop until you have a client base that will sustain a full-time profession.

Use this book as a resource for coaching yourself towards a more fulfilled life. It will help you to reach the goals you have dreamed of and show you how to remove any beliefs that have prevented you from achieving your desires. To use the book as a personal self-development tool, you should read the chapters in sequence and practise each technique in turn until it is mastered.

Read on to explore the fascinating and rewarding world of life coaching. I should warn you that it is easy to become a life coach. Even as you read this handbook you will begin to think, feel and act like a coach. From there it is one small step to a future as a professional life coach of excellence.

Section 1

The Coaching Process

Chapter One

Life Coaching Defined

'The first step towards success is knowing what it is that you aim to do'

Synopsis

Life coaching is a career and an ethical profession. The life coach uses the power of commitment to enable their clients to achieve beneficial and measurable results in all areas of their lives. Life coaching is a holistic process that has the power to balance and harmonise life.

Coaching. Is it a new phenomenon or an old profession dressed up to look exciting? Life coaching is one and both at the same time. It uses some of the skills of the old coaching styles combined with innovation. It concentrates on the person's whole life instead of just one area.

Conventional coaching tends to be specific in its approach. This means that the coach specialises in one profession or a single specialised area of expertise. Physical or sports coaches, for example, usually come from within that profession. They have proved their success as a professionally-paid player or athlete. In tennis, the best coaches of the top-ranking players have themselves been tennis professionals.

Football also follows this pattern. In the major leagues the coaches have come from the field of football, literally. These, then, are examples of the traditional types of coach. They design the physical training programmes and coach their clients accordingly. They have expertise and experience in the skill required. Then they endeavour to advise and coach their protégés in this skill.

During the 1980s the business coaches arrived in the guise of management or financial consultants. They are specialists in the business world who are usually hired when profits are going down. They have a role when companies have been through re-engineering, or a new product is to be launched. They are retained on a temporary basis, for instance, when a company identifies some missing skills that may not justify a permanent addition to staff. Consultants usually spend their time establishing facts, preparing reports, designing the new process or procedure and helping the client to implement approved proposals.

Management consultants contribute at least 75 per cent of the plan of action. The same contribution levels of 75 per cent, or more, are found in the sports-coaching role.

Life coaching is the converse of this: at least 75 per cent of the action plan comes from the client. An expert in a particular field can do life coaching but someone who has no specific knowledge of the skills required can just as effectively perform it. Indeed, some of the most successful life coaches do not have the expertise in the specialist fields of their clients.

Expertise in many trades or professions is not the role of the life coach. Laura Berman Fortgang, life coach and author of *Take Yourself to the Top*, writes, "I am your partner," and adds, "coaching is holistic." Another life coach, Eileen Mulligan, wrote in *Life Coaching – change your life in seven days*, "Life coaches are there to push you to change your life for the better." There is no mention in either book about the need for qualifications or expertise in any given field beyond that of life coaching itself.

So what is a life coach? Some life coaches believe that it is about advising clients. Some believe that it involves guiding clients to find their own answers. A few claim that you must have expertise within the fields where you coach. Spiritually focused life coaches say that it is all about "connection." Life coaches with therapy backgrounds believe that the process includes counselling or therapy.

In reality, life coaching can be all of the above. It depends on the needs of each individual client and the skills of the coach. When you use the techniques offered here, you can develop your own style and proficiencies to become a highly sought-after life coach.

Despite this diversity of approach, most life coaches agree that it is about achieving results. Most people, if asked, "Is there something you've been thinking about doing but have yet to start or complete?" will answer, "Yes." Then they will tell you exactly what it is and how long they have wanted to do it. They may even give you all the reasons why they have not done it. The life coach closes the gap between *thinking* about doing and actually doing.

Clients tend to underperform because there is conflict between their desires and their value systems. They depend on these values and belief systems for guidance, although many, developed in their childhood, may no longer serve them in adulthood. Nevertheless, people still judge and act by these obsolete principles.

Some life coaches seek to address these barriers before working with the client's desired outcomes. In the long term, any conflict between desires and beliefs should be investigated but, initially, the job of the life coach is to get results – results, results and nothing but results!

A life coach who spends initial time with clients on anything other than results will diminish the impact of the coaching process by converting it from a client-and-coach relationship to a client-and-therapist situation. This is not on the life coaching agenda.

When the life coach focuses on results or outcomes and enables their clients to define and achieve these with ease, then the clients can eventually be guided to examine their beliefs and values. It is not a primary function of the life coach to change the client's beliefs and values. Although changes in negative or undesirable values and beliefs can accelerate the achievement of outcomes, such changes should be addressed only with care and after a solid working relationship has been developed.

The main role of the life coach is to enable and empower the client. This is achieved using the "power of commitment" as leverage. Once clients agree to an activity they are committed to do it. This commitment is powerfully linked with the client's identity. The life coach taps into this power.

The power of commitment relies on the social reinforcement of people conforming to who they say they are. It uses the power of honesty. Clients become dishonest if they do not fulfil their commitment to the coach. Humans are conditioned to believe that people who do not fulfil their commitments are not to be trusted. They are seen as shifty, unreliable and devious, as liars and cheats. Clients do not want their life coach to think they are any of these so they will move heaven and earth to achieve the actions, goals and targets that they have agreed.

Guilt is another factor in the power of commitment. When clients do not achieve the goal, they punish themselves with guilt. This self-flagellation gives them far more pain than anything the coach can inflict. Humans usually have a driving need for pleasure and a driving need to avoid pain. The pain-and-pleasure continuum used as a powerful leveraging tool can ensure that clients achieve results. It is a simple process but a highly effective one in getting breakthroughs for the client.

Life coaching helps clients in every aspect of their lives. Unlike sports coaching or business consultancy, it is holistic and considers every dimension of a client's life. This includes business, career, health, social relationships, wealth and worth in contribution. If life coaching concentrates on just one area in isolation, and develops only that area, then the client's life can become unbalanced. When clients overachieve at work but underachieve in personal relationships, the negative effects of their personal relationships can adversely affect their performance at work.

When clients exceed in business success, but ignore their health, they can develop ulcers or serious illnesses. In the cyclical pattern of life, this means that they must take time away from the business and the business may suffer as a consequence. The life coach can advantageously use this effect when persuading high achievers to look to their health and the contribution areas of their lives.

Conversely, if clients focus on their physical body to the extent that they miss or skip work in order to maintain the body beautiful, they may end up with financial problems. Financial problems will cause them to worry and lose sleep. Loss of sleep will have an adverse impact on their body beautiful and this angle can be the coach's leverage to encourage these clients to focus on financial matters. Life is wonderfully cyclical, which gives the life coach great areas of persuasion when finding compelling reasons for clients to follow through on actions that will lead to achievement of goals in all areas of their lives.

Bringing balance and achievement into the lives of their clients produces rewards for the life coach, too. Helping clients to define goals in each life area and then working to help them to achieve results also brings an awareness of the importance of balance and harmony into the coach's life.

Life coaching is a relationship of interdependency between coach and client. It is a relationship based on honesty, respect and the life coach's unwavering beliefs in the client's unlimited potential.

Summary

- The physical or sports coach specialises in the body and a specific sport
- The business consultant defines problems, provides answers and helps to implement them within the business environment
- Life coaching focuses on results, results and nothing but results
- Life coaching works on all areas and aspects of life
- The power of commitment is the accelerator of success

Chapter Two

Life Coaching Explained

*'Life Coaching removes the interference that stands
between clients and the achievement of their potential'*

Synopsis

**It is your job as the life coach to help to identify the interference
and remove it. It has nothing to do with giving advice or imposing knowledge on your clients. Life coaching is about removing
the obstructions and not adding any new ones. Concentrate on
balancing all the areas of your clients' lives. Believe that your
clients have all the resources they need to solve their own problems and that it is your job to help them remove the obstacles
that prevent this happening.**

In the book *The Inner Game of Tennis* Tim Gallwey states that coaching can be outlined with the formula, "Potential minus Interference
equals Performance." It is your job as a life coach to help your
client to identify the interference and remove it. That's it!

Life coaching has absolutely nothing to do with giving advice, and
this can be tough on you when you know the answer. And, more
often than not, you *will* know the answer. Your strength lies in
allowing your clients to find the answers for themselves.

This is good news for coaches because giving advice is not as easy
as it seems. The advice-giving route carries huge responsibilities. If
you think you always have to supply an answer, you will become
very stressed and burdened with unnecessary troubles.

To ensure that you grasp the importance of this point, let me
repeat: coaching is not about *advising* your clients. Many of the
most outstanding coaches have little or no knowledge or experience in the areas where they coach their clients. This absence of

knowledge provides a clean sheet for the client to work *with* and *for* the coach and eliminates limiting beliefs about the client's potential or problems. Limiting beliefs are a main component of interference and are covered in Chapter Four.

Also, coaching is not about imposing knowledge or information on your clients. You must master your desire to tell your clients how they should do something. An outstanding coach elicits the answers from the clients as they guide them towards self-discovery. This may sound strange but, if you truly believe that your clients have all the resources they need, then all you have to do is to help them find the best pathway to successful results. Your clients will always be more committed to ideas and plans that they propose for themselves.

So life coaching is simple. All you have to do is to remove the obstructions without adding new ones as you concentrate on helping your clients to gain balance in all areas of their lives.

The obstructions are different for every client and also for every coach. It is these differences that make coaching such fun and such a challenge. An obstruction is anything that prevents your clients from achieving their potential for greatness. The biggest obstruction will be your clients' belief systems. Chapter Four deals solely with matters of belief. Here are some common types of obstructions that you will encounter while coaching.

No clear vision or mission. Your clients don't have a vision, a clear picture of what they want, or a mission statement (a sentence or two about who they are and what they stand for). Successful coaching relies on your clients determining exactly what they want to achieve in your coaching sessions or in their life.

Outcomes obscured. Some clients may come to you with several goals or outcomes. If they do not sound committed to achieving one of the outcomes it is possible that it belongs to their partner or another family member and is not their own. You must help your clients identify what they want and how they will personally gain once their own outcomes are achieved.

Self last. My definition of selfless is "less for the self." These clients are martyrs. You will have to work hard on reframing. Tell your clients the airline rule whereby, to ensure the child's best chance of survival, parents are ordered to put the oxygen mask on themselves prior to placing one on the child. Ask how their entire family will benefit when your client is healthy, wealthy, happy and whole. Giving precious time to develop and attain health and wealth goals to secure the future for the whole family is true selflessness.

Age barriers. Some clients say they would like to do something and then immediately dismiss the goal because of age. They feel too old (or too young) to start. You need to understand that. Even so, they do still have dreams and goals. It is your job to encourage your clients to realise their dreams. Start by considering the more easily achieved objectives that they may attempt. Your intention is to get them weaned on success and ultimately hooked so that they continue to work on their original dream. Today, as I write this chapter, a 90-year-old man is running in the London Marathon. He doesn't believe in ageism.

Financial problems. Clients may come to you for help in solving their financial problems. You must make it absolutely clear that you are not a financial adviser and that any action agreed between you and your clients is done without obligation or liability. Ask your client to spend time identifying their outgoings and income without prejudice. The next step is for them to consult a qualified financial adviser. Explain that you will be there to help them once they have clear actions, set by their financial adviser. Do not offer financial advice or recommend ways of solving their financial crisis or you could be leaving yourself open to risk of prosecution. You should be aware that there are stringently applied laws that govern the provision of financial advice, either free or in return for a fee. The whole area is a minefield and the safest coaching position is to stay away. You can and should, however, guide your clients towards discovering their own solutions.

Family commitments. This obstacle is the regular cherry. Your clients will use it to opt out of their dreams. It is your job to help them balance the needs and demands of their families with their guilty conscience and their true and ultimate destiny. Never let

11

clients use this obstacle. Help them understand that their dreams can be achieved without their families suffering. Show them how, by achieving their own dreams, their families will also benefit.

Hero syndrome. These clients always take on too much work. You need to uncover the reasons behind this action. Is it because they cannot say no? If this is the reason, recommend some really good books on assertiveness or suggest that they attend a short course where they will get the opportunity to practise the art of saying no. The other reason for accepting too much work is that they want to be seen as a hero. This is similar to the martyr – except that the hero enjoys the glory of being able to help and will willingly sacrifice themselves for the greater cause. If this is the underlying reason you could ask questions to expose this. Then move on to encourage exploration of alternative ways of experiencing the same feelings through achievement of your clients' outcomes and goals.

Lottery madness. "One day my numbers will come up." You need to get your clients to contemplate the true value of time and the here and now. Ask them what they could be doing towards their dreams right now. If you have a client who wants to own a house with a sea view, what could they do today, even in a small way, to help achieve the dream? For example, they could investigate the costs of this type of house; they could inspect the proposed location of the house or make a long-term plan that includes all the small tasks that must be done to help them achieve the dream. You might gently point out that, by putting their faith for the future in the notoriously long lottery odds, they are surrendering their ultimate freedom. This is the freedom to assume control of their lives by taking positive action that achieves the results that they desire.

Treading the treadmill. If your clients are in a rut and cannot see a way out, ask them to make a list of all the jobs, careers or professions that they could do if they had no restrictions. Explain that they must write all ideas down, as you want a very long list. They should send you a copy of the list before the next coaching session. Their next exercise is to prioritise the list in order of "ease to accomplish," "cost-effectiveness," "impact on family" and "impact on self". The client then gives each idea a mark between one and four for each of these four categories and then a simple total for each idea. Sixteen is the maximum score for any one idea and four is the minimum score. Those with the lowest scores are the priority ideas to start working on.

You must guide your client to discover their task prioritisation. Simply ask open questions until they decide which ideas they can adopt. Then coach them towards achieving the change. If your client finds this concept difficult, you can simply copy the form below and let them have it as a guide.

List your ideas in the first column. Mark each idea from 1–4.
1 for low (i.e. easy to do, low cost, little effort)
4 for high (i.e. hard to do, high costs, huge effort)
The best choice has the lowest marks

Ideas	Ease to do	Cost	Effect on family	Effect on self	Totals	The best choice

Time priorities. These clients come back time and time again without completing a task because they "did not have the time." This is not normally a genuine time issue: it is a commitment obstruction. Genuine time issues are easily addressed by recommending that your clients attend a time-management course or read a book on time management. If you unearth a commitment issue, you must confront your client with their behaviour and remind them of the commitment they have made to themselves and to you. Remind them of the benefits that they said they would enjoy when they achieved their goal. Challenge them on why they consistently fail to deliver.

Hooked on adrenaline. Several of your clients may be burning out because they work too hard and play too little. They get their kicks from the adrenaline rush of a crisis. They claim that they perform better when they have tight deadlines. They love the buzz and they may not want to give it up. Assure these clients that the buzz of achieving their goals through their own efforts is an equally strong but healthy and lasting euphoria. You will need to use some of the advanced techniques covered in Chapter Eight on Neuro-Linguistic Programming and Chapter Seventeen, which deals with the Spiral Coaching model.

Trapped by trappings. The client wants to lead a simpler life but feels unable to live without the material things that their current lifestyle provides. Ask these clients to write a list of all the reasons why they want a simpler life and all the reasons for remaining in the current lifestyle. Follow up by using a priority list similar to the one described earlier in **Treading the treadmill**. Coaching is about helping your clients to achieve balance with all areas of life. For these clients, their fixation on materialism is tipping the balance.

Sapped by suckers. Some clients keep company with people who take the juice and energy out of them. These friends, colleagues, sport partners and even spouses continually suck the enthusiasm out of such clients by creating obstacles or excuses to prevent change. Ask your client to consider the possibility that their associates may feel threatened by the planned changes and may need to be reassured, by the client, that change will be good for all parties. If this reassurance does not work, they may need to make some serious decisions about the value of these friendships. Support and encourage your client to find new friendships in the areas of their goals. Explain that they should spend time wisely and with people who will help, rather than hinder, them. This transition may take some time, since certain clients will not want to surrender old friends for new ideas. A seamless and successful way to accomplish this transition is to agree constantly to tasks that encourage forming new friendships that leave little time for activities with the old, nonsupportive friends and that encourage the remaining small amount of time to be spent with only the old friends who are positive-minded.

Rebel rebels! Rebels have loads of things they want to do but, as soon as they commit to you, they feel the burning desire to kick back at you by not achieving. Strange but true. I know this because I used to be a rebel against myself. Once I had committed to achieving tasks with my life coach, I would deliberately not do them. We worked out a great system to overcome this destructive trait. I would commit to only one or two tasks, but I could do more if I wanted. At the same time, I could even choose not to do anything. All the possible tasks were listed with the complete understanding that I might not do any of them. This created the freedom for me to achieve without the feeling of being forced to do things. This technique is being used at this moment, as I choose to spend my Sunday writing instead of feeling I *have* to write.

Life coaching is about removing the obstacles and encouraging your clients to go beyond their perceived barriers to the accomplishment of their dreams and aspirations. It is about using communication skills to get the best from your clients and to help them to identify the obstacles in their daily life. The aim is for them to create a life that is full of balance and fulfilment. It is about being there for your clients when everyone else thinks they are mad, bad or sad. It is understanding that all your clients have immense potential that is just waiting to be released. It is about knowing that you, as a coach, can help.

Summary

- Tim Gallwey states – "Potential minus Interference equals Performance"
- The biggest obstruction will be clients' belief systems
- The main obstacles are: No clear vision or mission; Outcomes obscured; Self last; Age barriers; Financial problems; Family commitments; Hero syndrome; Lottery madness; Treading the treadmill; Time priorities; Hooked on adrenaline; Trapped by trappings; Sapped by suckers; Rebel rebels!
- Be there for your clients when everyone else thinks they are mad, bad or sad

Chapter Three

Coaching versus Counselling and Therapy

*'Counsellors and therapists may look to the past for answers.
Life coaches deal with the now and the future'*

Synopsis

There are links between therapies and life coaching but the links are not in the style, methodologies, techniques or tools of working: they derive from cause and effect. Even if they have the ability for intervention, life coaches should always refer clients believed to need therapeutic help to fully trained and qualified professionals. Life coaching and therapy have very different agendas for the client. There is no officially recognised UK body for professionally qualified life coaches.

To identify the differences between coaching, counselling and therapy, it is necessary to present an overview of the procedures that are sometimes mistakenly confused with coaching. These typically include counselling, physiotherapy, psychotherapy, Neuro-Linguistic Programming (NLP), hypnotherapy and psychiatry.

Take physiotherapy and coaching. At first glance there is no obvious link between them, although using one therapy might lead to using the other. Physiotherapy is, according to *Chambers Twentieth Century Dictionary*, "treatment of disease ...." This has nothing whatsoever to do with life coaching. Life coaching does not deal with diseases of the body or mind. It does help with clients' *dis-ease*, unease or dissatisfaction. It helps with issues of self-esteem and inability to achieve desired goals.

There may be a possible link of cause and effect. If, for example, a client comes to you for support and encouragement while they are receiving treatment from their physiotherapist. Then your coaching could take the form of motivating the client to keep performing the exercises recommended by their physiotherapy programme. By encouraging and congratulating the client on the improvements made and then helping them to set new targets, your coaching can have a huge impact on their speed of recovery.

The reverse of this is less pleasant. It could occur after you have encouraged your client to take up some form of exercise to improve their health. If, under your guidance and encouragement, they overstretch themselves and suffer injury, they may require the assistance of a physiotherapist. Do note, however, that these are simple "cause-and-effect" links. There are no links that concern the methods of working.

All of the other therapies mentioned generally involve some form of personal-history analysis. The client ordinarily has to go into their past for the therapist to devise a method of treatment. Thus the therapists need extensive knowledge and ability if they are to offer useful advice. Counselling, for example, may be needed following a single and clearly identified trauma such as bereavement, serious accident to self or family, divorce or redundancy.

Life coaching, however, is based in the present and the future. It is founded on the premise that the past need not equate to the future. Most coaches do not advocate giving advice to clients, preferring to work as a catalyst in helping clients to define their own way forward. This is a very different method of working from those used by a therapist or counsellor.

Many counsellors and psychotherapists are drawn to a career in life coaching. This presents serious challenges for them because coaching differs from the way that they have become accustomed to dealing with their patients. The decision to call them a 'patient' or 'client' helps to distinguish intervention from guidance.

Generally speaking, both these professions explore the patient's past by discovering previously created blocks or obstacles. Then they use interventions to remove these blocks or obstacles to help the patient's recovery. They use techniques and language patterns that are designed and dedicated for this approach.

These methods are not needed in life coaching. Indeed they could present problems for the coaching client who may become confused and misunderstand the vital distinction between therapy and life coaching – that therapy works from the past and life coaching starts from the present.

Life coaching is not about the past, which is important only if it seriously affects the results of the coaching. In such instances the life coach would refer the client to a specialist therapist for help, as it is not part of coaching to offer therapeutic interventions.

Even if the life coach, like myself, has the appropriate therapy skills and qualifications to do this, it is still preferable for the client to seek help from other professional sources. The reason for this recommendation is that clients can easily become confused about whether their sessions are therapy or coaching, and this can irrevocably damage the relationship.

The serious implication of attempting to combine therapy with life coaching is that a confused client may find no benefits from either. If the client needs therapy and becomes disillusioned because of this confusion of boundaries, there is a risk they may never again seek or receive the assistance that they need to live a fulfilling and rewarding life.

This is a very serious burden for the therapist and should be avoided at all costs. So, to summarise, a therapist should stick to therapy during a session and a life coach should stick to coaching. The therapist can then continue looking towards the past with the life coach dealing with the present and the future.

Life coaching has *absolutely no connections* with psychiatry. Should a life coach suspect that a client might have a need for such specialist attention, they should not attempt a diagnosis. They should firmly and gently tell the client to consult their doctor, who is trained to diagnose a problem and to recommend psychiatry or other treatment.

NLP includes some very useful techniques for life coaching. The NLP section of this book identifies these, with the emphasis on the linguistic aspects. It also covers some of the neurological features the life coach can use. It deliberately excludes therapeutic interventions. Life coaching is *not* about interventions. It is about goal setting and achievement.

There are currently no formally recognised professional qualifications for life coaching. This means that anyone – a carpenter, a tarot reader, a doctor or a preacher could put a sign outside their door, BEWARE OF THE LIFE COACH, and then start to advertise and practise life coaching.

There are several good organisations that offer training leading to their own qualifications in life coaching. Training is delivered at day or residential courses, distance learning via the Internet or, in some instances, a combination of both. It is important for all life coaches to obtain some form of qualification, which clients can check and verify if they are so minded. All coaches should advocate the importance of thorough training and qualifications and the adherence to a stringent code of ethics to protect the reputation of this still young, but fast growing, profession.

Summary

- Types of therapy: physiotherapy, counselling, psychotherapy, Neuro-Linguistic Programming, hypnotherapy and psychiatry
- Treatment of disease has nothing whatsoever to do with life coaching
- Life coaching is based in the present and the future
- The life coach must refer special-need clients to a qualified professional

Chapter Four

Essential Coaching Beliefs

'We are what we choose to believe we are'

Synopsis

It is essential for all coaches to understand how beliefs are formed and the impact that they have on themselves and their clients. This understanding ensures that we perform at our best and elicit the best performances from our clients. Without this understanding you can waste precious time working on areas that are controlled by a client's fundamental belief. Use the "self-talk interrupt" process to help your clients. Using role models needs good questioning skills to determine the client's underlying beliefs. Recommend a therapist for significant belief changes and concentrate on coaching.

It is essential for every life coach to understand how beliefs are formed and the impact that they have on clients and coaches alike. This understanding will ensure that you perform at your best and elicit the best results from your clients. Without this understanding, you will waste precious time on areas that are controlled by a fundamental client belief.

Your beliefs were being formed from the moment you entered this world. People smiled or shouted at you when you were a baby. These, and all your subsequent interactions with other humans, formed the person that you are today. You have created, and continue to create, an image of yourself that is based on the attitudes of other people. It is an image that can either help or hinder the development of your potential and it changes with circumstances and situations.

At the beginning of your life, "experts" evaluated everything that you did. You accepted and recorded their opinions as the truth.

These experts were your parents, teachers and elders and may even have included the village idiot. Now that you are grown up you can evaluate whether these well-meaning souls really were experts concerning your abilities. You can decide whether they added to or limited your development. They probably did both.

You now operate within the limits of your self-image and it becomes real for you. Eventually it becomes your comfort zone, where you feel safe, secure and protected. A comfort zone can be a negative place. You can feel safe and secure in prison but you would surely not want to stay incarcerated for ever.

Many people, perhaps you too, choose to stay in the prison of self-image, self-beliefs and self-talk. In the British penal system the authorities will release you as soon as you have served your sentence. All that it takes to escape from your *mentally created* prison is your decision to change.

As soon as you decide to change, you have the freedom to choose and to enjoy empowering beliefs and behaviours. The process is the same for your clients. They have their own imagined prisons and it is your job to provide the key that allows them to open the door and enjoy freedom.

Remaining within an imagined prison – to retain beliefs and to repeat behaviours while expecting a different outcome – can be compared to a trapped wasp. It will continue to fly into the windowpane, time and time again until it dies. It never looks for alternative escape routes. It just keeps flying at the glass. Performing the same task in the same way and expecting different results has been offered as a definition of madness. With total self-honesty, you may admit that you have probably done just this and you are still getting the same results.

Your self-image is an accumulation of every attitude and opinion that you have been told about yourself since birth. You have perpetuated and reinforced this by repetition until, eventually, it has formed the subconscious picture of your self-image. This has become who you believe that you are, it determines how you respond to life and what you believe you are capable of doing. It has become your comfort zone.

This comfort zone is the life that you are comfortable to live. It could even be full of pain, poverty and drudgery. People remain in these situations because their self-image and belief systems support them there. They feel secure and comfortable in the knowledge that this is what they deserve or are worthy of.

You are within a closed loop. Your self-image is created by your belief system (what you believe to be true about yourself). You build and nourish these beliefs and feel comfortable with them. They become who you believe you are. You know and trust them because you can prove that they are right and, therefore, they must be true.

The loop has three components:

- how you behave
- your self-talk
- your picture of self-image

As you move from one to the next you simply reinforce and strengthen each stage in a never-ending cycle.

Think of a belief as an empty suitcase. Once you have a suitcase you can find clothes to pack into it. Everything that has been said *to* you, *about* you, becomes a piece of clothing. Everything that has been done to you becomes another piece of clothing – a reference for you to put into the suitcase.

All the references that you can find in your life become the clothes to pack. Soon, you have a very strong and very full suitcase. The more clothes (references) that you cram into the suitcase (belief), the more certain you become about your belief (life). More references equal stronger beliefs, which you continue to nurture because they make you sure about who you are.

Your beliefs can be changed. Your clients' beliefs can be changed. You can start right now to change any limiting or disabling beliefs that are holding you back from becoming who you were created to be. The following practical, simple exercise will allow you to prove this for yourself. Do it now.

First, identify your own limiting beliefs. For example, you may believe, "I am too old," "I am too young," "I don't have a university degree," "I am too fat." Listen for the things that you think you know are true about you. Think of these in the context of situations that make you feel helpless, unsure, inadequate, lacking in confidence.

Now select just one of these limiting beliefs. Find all the references that support it (the clothes in your suitcase). Find as many references as you can and list them all.

Here is where the fun begins. Decide to believe something different. This should be the opposite view. For example, if you had the limiting belief that, "I am bad at remembering names," just decide that, from now on, your belief will be, "I am good at remembering names."

Once you have created a sentence that states your new positive belief you can repeat it over and over again. This constant repetition will enhance your self-image and will break into the closed loop of your belief systems.

It may have taken you all your life to acquire your old, limiting belief. So be prepared for it to take some time for the new liberating belief to cut in. You may need to repeat this sentence frequently and even repeat the whole process. Whenever you find yourself thinking your old belief, repeat your new positive version to yourself.

Your positive sentences must contain three essential components. Make them personal by using the word "I." Make them in the present tense by using the word "am." Include a positive description such as, "a great singer."

Here are a few more examples

- I am a good cook
- I am a great football player
- I am a calm person
- I am a person who says what needs saying
- I am a brilliant mathematician

- I am happy
- I feel terrific
- I am a great speller
- I am slim
- I am good at ironing
- I am a great letter writer
- I am a magician

The last step in this exercise is to write down three positive statements about yourself. They do not need to be true just yet – they are statements that you would *like* to be true about you and that could become true. As before, you must use the present tense, as if they were already true.

Use these statements to replace the equivalent, old, limiting belief. Add the references to support these new, positive and empowering beliefs.

Create a mental image of yourself actually doing and enjoying this new behaviour. This will gradually create your new self-image. This is the new vision of how you really are.

The next time that you find yourself behaving in the old (limiting) way, or even thinking in that way, you must stop that voice in your head and replace it immediately with your new sentence – even if it is not yet true. What you are doing here is recognising the old pattern, interrupting and breaking it, and then replacing it with your empowering belief. This is called the "self-talk interrupt" process.

- You must *stop the old voice* immediately it starts.
- Replace it with your *new sentence* even if it is not yet true.
- See, feel and *experience the rewards* of your new belief. Enjoy these rewards as if you already had them.

You really do have a choice. You can give up and carry on reinforcing your old limiting beliefs or you can play your new, empowering sentence and work on changing your beliefs.

Find something that you already do well and praise yourself for that skill. Then build on that praise by adding your new sentence.

If any negative thoughts enter your mind, say to yourself, "Erase that thought, I am ..." and add your new sentence. Concentrate on repeating the new belief about yourself.

You choose to believe your own beliefs, therefore you can choose to change them.

The motivational speaker Anthony Robbins of Robbins Research International says, "It is in your moments of decision that your destiny is shaped." One of your key moments of decision is when you decide not to believe in limiting beliefs and then help your clients to do the same.

Here is a very powerful and easy way to change old habits and beliefs. Think of a person whom you consider to be very skilful in what it is that you want to be able to do. Now model that person. Stand in front of a mirror (in private) and mimic the ways they hold their body, talk, laugh, breathe, move and anything else you can think of.

Consider how they get what they want, how they stand, sit, walk, gesticulate. Think about what they do that you currently do not do. Then ask this question, "What would I need to believe in order to behave in this same way?" When you and your client know the answer to this question, the key to developing the desired skill is within your reach.

Use this technique to help you to develop yourself and your clients. When your clients name a person they wish to emulate, you must examine the underlying reasons behind their choice of this model. What is the skill that they wish to acquire and does the model have it in abundance? Is it truly the skill that they desire or simply their model's lifestyle? Ask them to think of others who have the desired skill, as this opens up their possibilities and allows them really to explore their desire for it. The crucial question that must always be answered is, "What does the model have to believe in order to have success in that skill?"

Practising these belief-changing techniques will help you to know that they work. Once you believe in the success of a technique you are able to make it available to your client with sincerity and assurances that it really is effective.

Some of your clients may have attended personal development courses or seminars and will have heard about limiting beliefs. When this happens you can simply weave belief-changing suggestions into your normal coaching sessions. Clients who have no prior knowledge will need to be very carefully guided through the whole subject of belief changing, as it can be difficult to grasp when it is first heard. You may wish to write out the belief-changing exercise and ask such clients to complete it for discussion at a later session.

A more beneficial approach would be to suggest that your client consult an NLP practitioner or therapist for help in belief changing.

Remember that you are employed as a coach, not as a therapist. You must not confuse the boundaries, because this will weaken your coaching sessions and damage your reputation as an outstanding results-oriented life coach.

Remember that *coaching is only about results*.

Summary

- Beliefs are formed from the moment we connect with others
- Limiting beliefs can restrict your performance as a coach
- Listen to negative self-talk and interrupt the pattern
- Models also have beliefs – ask the questions
- Recommend a therapist for fundamental belief changes

Chapter Five

Essential Communication Skills

'How to say what you mean when you mean what you say'

Synopsis

Communication includes body language, tonality of voice and the words you use. Good listening supplies the building blocks of good understanding. Open questions encourage clients to think positively for themselves and to give an original, genuine answer. Restrict your use of closed questions to times when you have facts and details to check. An open question is often more useful.

The ability to listen to, observe and interpret all forms of language is essential for life coaching. Several different studies on how we communicate show that, if both people are totally congruent at the time of communicating, some 55 per cent of their communication will be by body language, approximately 38 per cent will be based on tonality of voice and only 7 per cent will derive from the words themselves.

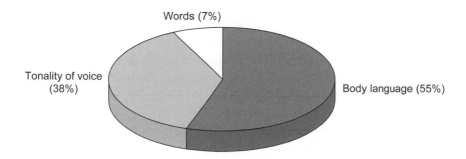

Recently the validity of using these results or the results of similar studies in relation to general communication has been questioned. However, when you are coaching, it is important to make sure that your words, body language and tonality are congruent. Congruency means that they are all aligned and sending the same message.

This means that, if you say yes when your head is moving from side to side, even the slightest movement will be interpreted from your body language as meaning no. We have all experienced conversations where we have come away thinking, "I'm not so sure that they meant what they said." This is probably a result of reading one message from their body language that was incongruent with their totally different verbal message.

It is also important that you maintain eye contact when you are talking to your clients, as this is a natural expression of your interest in their message. Avoid closing your eyes in conversation as this breaks the eye contact and distracts the client's attention. It may even cause them to think that you are not to be trusted. Similarly, if you consistently look away while either of you is speaking, the client may interpret, rightly or wrongly, that you are shifty, deceitful, untrustworthy or just plain rude.

Your body language tells your clients what you are thinking about them and you must send a message of openness, honesty and trust. This can be achieved only by open body language, with your arms either open and relaxed at your side or resting comfortably on your lap.

Do not cross your arms or legs during a conversation with a client. They could interpret this posture as meaning that you are not interested in what they have to say or that you feel insecure and nonassertive. No client will feel reassured or confident with your coaching abilities when they have these thoughts. Remember, you have no control over how your client interprets your body language.

If your practice is in an area with a high proportion and mix of ethnic residents, you should undertake some personal research on any particular body-language gestures that are especially respectful, acceptable or downright rude in other cultures.

The nineteenth-century American philosopher and poet Ralph Waldo Emerson said, "What you are doing speaks so loudly I can't hear what you say." Clients glean a lot of information about you from your tone of voice, and vice versa. Sometimes your coaching sessions with your clients will be conducted over the telephone. At such times you need to be particularly aware of your tonality, which will transmit a major portion of your message.

Tone conveys:

- your social class
- your district and country of origin
- your current emotional state
- your physical state
- your attitude towards the other person

If your natural speaking voice sounds monotonous you must change it by adding some high and low notes to make your tone richer and more interesting for your listener. Engage the services of a speech therapist or a voice coach if you need to. If you speak too softly, your clients may interpret it as lack of confidence or drive. Be aware of any changes that you need to.make to the volume of your voice to convey the messages you want to convey.

You will find it useful to listen regularly to interviews on speech radio. Unlike television encounters, where the images may distract you, radio interviews will help you to identify what makes a voice "boring" or "interesting." Then, armed with this information, you can compare your own normal voice and make any necessary corrections. You will find a small tape recorder very useful for this.

Good breathing will help you to control volume and tonality. If you breathe deeply when you are speaking, you can actually give yourself more voice power. You can gradually – or, for effect, suddenly – increase the speed, then speak quickly, and then slow down again, all within a few sentences.

Voice inflections can change the emphasis of what you say. Your tone can even change the meaning of a simple statement. For example, if your voice stays level all the way through a sentence it will imply to your clients that this is a statement. If you raise your voice at the end of a statement, it will be heard as a question. If, instead, you drop your voice at the end, it gives the impression of a command. If you are listening actively, you are receiving these tonality differences, too. Be conscious of what your voice tone is conveying and make sure you are congruent.

Trust your inner voice and your instinct when you are speaking. If you are unsure, start by saying, "I am unsure whether this is the right thing to say." An alternative is, "I have had this thought. Is that all right with you?"

Avoid using "try." It implies that you think that you will not succeed. Perhaps it even implies that it does not matter if you don't succeed because you didn't make a firm commitment to do something: you merely said you would try. Listen to your own language.

If you are using the word "try," you are setting yourself up for failure. Not just failure when dealing with clients but failure in dealing with yourself. You are giving your subconscious mind the message that it is acceptable to fail. It is not acceptable to fail. Exchange "try" for a more powerful word, one that will empower you and yield better results.

If you replace the word "try" with "will" you may still fail, but at least you have given yourself a greater chance of success. By saying "I will," you are giving your subconscious mind the instruction to succeed in this venture instead of merely to try, which is the instruction or excuse to fail. Use "will" and your subconscious will provide you with the resources needed for success, simply because you have flagged that outcome as important.

Listen for the use of "try" by your clients, because this tells you that their commitment level is not high enough to complete the task. As soon as a client says "I will try," immediately question the commitment by repeating, with a questioning inflection and a raised voice, the word "try?" – indicating you are asking them if "try" is all they are going to do. If they continue to use "try," ask, "On a scale of a hundred per cent, where's your commitment to this task at the moment?" If it is lower than 75 per cent, your client will not fulfil on this. Ask, "What would you need to do in order to increase your commitment to a hundred per cent?"

Another word to avoid when speaking with your clients is "but." When you hear the word "but" or "however," you automatically know the speaker has not listened to, does not agree with or is going to ignore completely what has just been said. Ask yourself how good you feel when you have said something and received the "but" or "however" response. This is not the feeling that you want to give your clients. Replace "but" with another three-letter word that is incredibly empowering. Your clients will feel that you have considered their viewpoint.

Replace "but" with "and." Then you are saying to your clients that you have listened to them and you would also like them to take into consideration what you are going to add. The client feels comfortable and picks up the impression that you had an interest in what they said. Indeed, they were so interesting that it inspired you to build on their comments with your own point of view.

Do Not Think of a Red Boat!

Now that you've read the above heading, what do you now have in your mind? It will be a picture of a red boat!

The reason for this is the English language. The mind cannot take a negative verb at the beginning until it knows what the actual object of the sentence is; then, by the time you get to the object, you have had to create it (in order not to create it!).

If you want people to do something, or if you want them to stop doing something, be very clear with your instructions. For example, tell someone, "Don't forget my book when you come to work tomorrow," and you are planting the suggestion and instruction to forget your book. To increase the chances of the book's arriving, just simply tell them what you want them to do. "Please remember to bring in my book tomorrow morning."

"Good morning!" said Bilbo and he meant it. The sun was shining, and the grass was very green. But Gandalf looked at him from under long bushy eyebrows that stuck out further than the brim of his shady hat.

"What do you mean?" he said. "Do you wish me a good morning, or mean that it is a good morning whether I want it or not; or that you feel good this morning; or that it is a morning to be good on?"

– The Hobbit, J.R.R. Tolkien

This extract shows that even a simple greeting like "good morning," can be taken in four different ways. In fact, "good morning" can also be used to say that you want to get rid of someone. Use a sharper, deeper tone of voice and it means that you want them to go. So, if words have several different interpretations, you need to take great care with the ones that you use during coaching sessions.

Listening is probably the most underrated communication skill. It is a critical element of any successful interaction with your clients. Good listening supplies the building blocks of good understanding.

You should listen to help you build a picture of your client's world, its information and its substance, and their experience of it. Listen for their potential and their obstacles. This involves listening to and interpreting what your clients are saying – and noting what is *not* being said. Recognise both verbal and nonverbal messages.

Listening is an active process involving:

ears – for verbal communications
eyes – for nonverbal communications
body – for physically showing that you are listening

Always practise active listening when you are coaching. At a face-to-face coaching session, sit square to and directly opposite your client. Turning at an angle from them will lessen your involvement. Adopt an open posture with your arms open and your palms upwards. Lean slightly forwards to show that you are very interested in them and what they are saying. The client must see that you are relaxed and in control of the situation.

Allow your client to confirm that you are listening by using encouraging noises such as, "I see," "Mmm," "Yes," and "Aha." These all allow your client to continue talking with the understanding that you are listening. During face-to-face sessions, use these noises in conjunction with nonverbal signals, such as nodding the head and looking expectant.

Well-timed pauses give time for explanation, evaluation and development of thought. Be sensitive to facial expressions to tell the difference between a pregnant pause and an embarrassed silence. Pauses on the telephone need to be constantly monitored so that your clients do not feel that they have to ask if you are still listening. Using active listening techniques will encourage your clients to confide in you and this will allow you to develop them further than they ever thought possible.

It is claimed by some researchers that over 2 million pieces of information reach our senses every minute. How this can be measured is a mystery to me but the reason I am mentioning this is because we filter information received so that it makes sense in our personal model of the world. We add, distort, assume and delete all of the time. For example, as you are reading these sentences your filters have deleted most of the environment around you to enable you to concentrate. These filters protect your mind and in doing so they sometimes hinder your abilities and progress. Think about this statement:

Pat Black, managing director of Security Systems Limited, called Les Millett to arrange a meeting.

About 80 per cent of readers will assume Pat is a male and about 60 per cent will also assume Les is male. There is nothing in the sentence to indicate the sex of either Pat or Les. What sex are your Pat and Les? Did you assume any of the following?

- Pat is male because of the position of managing director
- Pat is male because the company is a security company

- Pat is male because you know a male called Pat
- Pat is female because you know a female called Pat
- Les is male because Pat is male
- Les is Pat's female secretary

The problem for the coach is to listen without assuming, adding, deleting or distorting information received.

Summarising is an essential active coaching skill that serves to clarify the particular area under discussion and clearly demonstrates that you are listening. It involves reviewing the topic or theme you are considering by briefly restating the key elements. Regular summarising, including checking understanding, helps to reduce the impact of assuming meaning. State what you believe was expressed by saying, "My understanding of what you've just said is …" and clearly state all you believe to be true (Pat is male/female for example).

Summarising allows you to take stock of the main points already covered. It demonstrates understanding and separates what has been covered into "goals still under discussion" and "goals that remain unexplored." Summarising acts as a marker or reference point. When you use a summary to confirm your client's commitment to actions it increases the leverage for results.

Once a client has agreed to take action, ask them to set a date by which it will be accomplished. Listen for hesitation, a weak voice or lack of certainty, as these are indicators that your client is not fully committed to this action and will probably not do it. Whenever you hear hesitation you must confront your client to re-establish the outcomes or the purpose.

It is futile to let hesitation pass in the hope that your clients will complete the task simply because they said they would. Challenge your client: "I'm not convinced you're committed to doing [the agreed assignment]. On a scale of one to five, five meaning you're fully committed to making this happen, where would you say you are at the moment?" If your client says three or below, you can be sure they will not carry out the assignment. When clients do not achieve their agreed tasks it reflects badly on you. You are responsible for their results.

Questioning is an important skill for life coaches, because it can help you to discover your clients' ideas, thoughts, needs and problems. With effective questioning you can show care, interest, sympathy, empathy and your wish to help your clients to develop.

You can use questions to lead clients into thinking for themselves, thinking positively, solving their own problems and taking actions. All too often, we ask closed questions that invite a yes-or-no answer. These questions often start with a verb or verbal phrase:

*   Do you have any goals you want to work on?
*   Will you write to them if I give you the address?
*   Did you call the bank manager?
*   Do you work more effectively when I challenge you?
*   Do you want to have the meeting on Monday?
*   Can you send the cheque by first-class mail?
*   Do you want the Gold Service?

Closed questions are useful for checking detail, confirming facts and getting commitment to action. Take care, though, because they may produce a misleading answer or put the client into the position where they feel that they must answer **yes**, just to please you.

Open questions are the most effective type for coaching. They pass the control to your client and produce lots of useful information. There are seven main words for asking open questions:

Who can you approach to help you achieve that?
Where can you find that information?
Which goal is more important to you?
How far did you get with that task?
What date will you achieve this by?
When did you complete that?
Why is that important to you?

When you are seeking thoughts, feelings and reactions from your clients use such questions as:

How do you feel about …?
What do you think of …?

What happens when …?
What should we do about …?
What do you like about …?

"When" is often used to obtain factual answers from your clients, as it date-stamps actions and commitments: When did you complete the task? When will you complete the task?

"When" can be useful to lead the discussion towards decision-making time. Consider the usefulness of the "when" question for the following:

- getting a commitment
- planning a project
- gaining agreement from a client
- getting acceptance of your suggestion

"Why" seeks to ascertain the feelings or reactions of your clients. It can investigate their motivation, present a challenge or a threat, put your clients on the defensive or produce reasons and excuses.

Asking a "why" question runs the risk of producing an evasive, aggressive or uncooperative response from your clients. It is useful to replace "why" with "what" or "how." These will give you the same results without putting your clients into defensive mode. This is especially important if they have not achieved the agreed tasks. Consider the difference between "Why didn't you do it?" and "What stopped you from doing it?"

To answer the first question, your client has to justify their nonaction, which can build obstacles and resistance to doing the task. "What stopped you?" compels your client to search for the reasons without feeling any need to justify them.

Useful Questions (and Points) to Put to Your Clients

What do you want to get from having me as your coach?
What is it you think I can provide that you don't have yourself?
What is it that you want to accomplish?

What will it provide you with?
What else?
What steps do you think you can do to fulfil this?
When you say [X], what does that mean?
So is that like [Y]?
What else specifically?
How specifically?
What are you willing to do to make this happen?
How is life now?
Tell me more about that, please.
What would that look like?
What I don't understand is ...
Where in your life are you not doing [A]?
What concerns do you have about that?
How was that process for you?
What you want coaching on is [B].
How committed are you in this?
What makes this an issue for you?
Who makes you do [C]?
What does "happy" mean for you?
What would happen if you didn't ...?
Is that what you want?
If not now, when?
If not you, then who?
What is possible?
Are you willing to be open and honest with me?
What would you need to know to be able to ...?
What's missing?
What needs to be present for it to happen?
What is it about [X] that will give you ...?
What would it take for you to know rather than just thinking?
When will you have the experience?
How can you bring that into your life right now?
Would that make [Y] more fulfilling for you?
Would it work for you to do that today?
Where can you find a better way right now to get what you
    want?
When will you do that?
Are you clear about what we've agreed you will do?
What else do you want to work on?

What's your level of commitment to yourself on a scale of one
 to ten?
What do you think you need today?

Any question that gives you information, that makes your client
think or that reveals hidden motivations is a good question.

To some extent, it is better if you can encourage people to give you
information without having to ask too many questions. When
your client is responding, use encouraging noises or words.
Combining these with open questions can keep ideas and opinions
flowing:

Noises	Hmm
	Oh
	Aha
Phrases	I see
	Do go on
	That's right
	Good
	Tell me about …
Repetition of	Promotion next year?
key words	So Mr Jones needs to read it?
	Completed by the 15th?
Body language	Nod
	Raised eyebrows
	Lean forward
	Smile
	Concentrate on the answer
	Look interested
Questioning	Comments made in an enquiring tone, achieved
statements	by raising your voice at the end of the sentence:
	You do?
	That's all?
	It was really good?
	That's so?

Using encouraging signs and noises gives you more time and
space to think and consider the ideas being expressed. Even a
pause, if it is accompanied by positive body language, can be
encouraging and lead to an improved exchange of views.

Summary

- Studies show that body language and tone are more important than words
- Clients can pick up a lot of information about you from your tone of voice
- Good breathing will help you increase your volume and tonality
- Avoid using "but," "try," "don't" and "why"
- The art of questioning is an important skill for life coaches
- Listen for potential and obstacles

Chapter Six

How to Build a Coaching Practice

*'Creating clients is an art that requires your time,
your skills and your dedication'*

Synopsis

You must be able to generate enquiries and convert an enquiry into a paying client in order to stay in business. The two main areas the life coach initially needs to concentrate on are how to build the practice and how to get clients interested enough to pay for your service. Actually setting up a life coaching practice is very simple and inexpensive. The four things you need are a telephone, notepaper, diary and a pen. Using the RABIT model you can easily turn the enquiry into a paying client. Referrals are the most effective approach to building a client base and therefore building a successful coaching practice.

This is one of the most important chapters in this book. You must be able to generate enquiries and then convert an enquiry into a paying client in order to stay in business.

Without this skill you will not create your life coaching practice and will be robbed of that superb feeling of excitement that arrives when one of your clients succeeds beyond their wildest dreams.

You need to start by concentrating on two main areas: building your practice and getting clients interested enough to pay for your service. Many life coaches come from a heartfelt desire to help their fellow human beings and it is this desire that was their motivation to enter the profession.

The big dilemma for these life coaches is justifying to themselves the need to charge for this service. After all, they rationalise, "The client does all the work and I only facilitate the success." Always remember that clients pay for your experience, knowledge, training and background, which have all cost you a great deal more than the few hundred pounds that you will be charging for your coaching sessions.

Actually setting up a life coaching practice is very simple and inexpensive. Here are the only four things that you really need to begin.

- telephone
- notepaper or printed forms that you predesign
- pen or pencil
- diary

You can start your practice off with only these four items and it will work. When you add the following inexpensive items you will be off to a winning start.

ITEM	DESCRIPTION
A colour trifold brochure with a picture of you on the front or the back.	An A4 sheet of paper folded three ways, which describes the benefits of life coaching along with who you are and how to contact you. You will either hand these out or send them off to people who seek more information. With the owners' consent, you can place them in locations where your prospective clients are likely to visit.
Business cards	These should have your name, practice name, address and telephone number. Include your fax number, e-mail address and website details if you have them. Your business cards can be one of your most effective low-cost marketing tools, but they cannot work for you if they are sitting in your desk drawer.
Headed paper	Paper with your practice name, address and your logo. Keep to standard A4 size.
Compliments slips	Rectangular pieces of headed notepaper with "With compliments" printed in the centre. These are usually one-third of an A4 sheet.
Press releases	Typed press releases about life coaching. You send these regularly to local, national press and media to generate interest and clients. Remember to include your telephone number for any enquiries.

The majority of typical high street printers will be pleased to help you with design and content, and many of them offer attractively priced "business start-up packs." If you are working from your home, it can be advantageous to use a PO Box number as your address. This is easy to arrange with the post office. The cost is very low and you can choose whether your mail is delivered with your usual domestic post or whether you collect it from your local sorting office. You pay more to have it delivered.

You will also need to arrange a separate business bank account, bookkeeping, and VAT registration (optional). These matters will be dealt with in more detail in Chapter Eighteen.

So, how do you generate interest in an embryonic service-industry profession? Well, life coaching is about people and for people, so you *go* to the people.

A remarkably effective way of generating clients is to deliver talks and demonstrations anywhere that groups of people get together. Contact your local business groups such as the Chamber of Commerce, Institute of Management, women's groups, diners' clubs and the many organisations that meet regularly and invite external speakers.

This is a marvellous opportunity for you to explain and demonstrate your service. You can offer a prize of a couple of free coaching sessions to the organisation and this can produce money for them if they organise a raffle. Organisations or clubs always welcome offers of free gifts.

Plan your talk beforehand. It should have a structure and be timed exactly according to the time slot allocated. Introduce yourself as a professional life coach and always start with a big statement to catch the attention and imagination of your audience.

Think carefully about your audience and make your opening statement powerfully relevant to them. Then proceed with your talk, and include the benefits of life coaching and the benefits of using you, and do a short demonstration. Finally, the talk should summarise the main benefits you can offer them. Your powerful last sentence must link to your equally arresting opening. Here are three possibilities:

Opening: "Life coaching can seriously change your life."

Closing: "Call me only if you're serious about making the changes you've always wanted to make."

Opening: "Think of me as a bottle opener – I release your potential."

Closing: "Let me help you to pop your cork of potential."

Opening: "I am a magician. I reawaken dreams and make them come true."

Closing: "Life coaching is the millennium magic."

Inform your host that you will be asking for a volunteer to demonstrate life coaching. Get a commitment from your host that, if no volunteer comes from the floor, they will offer to be the one. It is important to demonstrate how powerful life coaching can be and to be able to answer any questions about it after the demonstration.

Plan what you are going to say and rehearse several times in front of friends. When asking for volunteers to take part in your demonstration simply ask your audience, "Is there anyone here who has an area in their life they've tried to change in the past but were not successful, and still wants to change that area?"

When you ask for volunteers, you may get several offers. Simply ask each of them to tell you one thing that they want to change. The intention here is for you to select a topic that you know you could handle and one that you believe will have a positive impact on your audience.

Before starting your demonstration say loudly, so that the whole audience can hear, "Thank you for volunteering. I want to give you two free coaching sessions after this demonstration as a thank-you gift. You'll all be aware that a brief demonstration will never replace the effectiveness of a full session. I really want [name of volunteer] to succeed with [their stated change]. To do this competently and professionally will take at least two full sessions. This demonstration will give you all only a brief introduction, an idea of how it works. The multitude of benefits that you'll get from life coaching sessions can be truly enjoyed only when you book a course of coaching with me. Coaching achieves outstanding results after only a few sessions have been experienced." (There are some embedded commands in the above sample speech – see Chapters Thirteen and Fourteen on language patterns.)

This sets the scene and prepares your audience to accept that you will not attempt to complete the process in the forum of a public demonstration. By confirming that you will finish the procedure later and at no charge to your volunteer, you will convey the message that you are a generous and professional coach.

If you have not spoken to a group of people before, you really need to get professional assistance by attending a course on presentations. There are some very good courses available on the market ranging from one day to several days. If you cannot afford to attend a course, look in your local directory for toastmaster or speaking clubs. There is an American Toastmasters organisation, which holds regular meetings for public speaking around the country; they will welcome you and train you at the same time.

You will also find it valuable to attend seminars and listen to as many other speakers and presenters as you can. You will learn a lot by watching and you will also observe a few poor techniques that you will want to avoid in your own presentations.

Another way to generate interest is to send a press release to your local newspaper about your new practice. They may publish a feature that has genuine human interest or news value but they will decline a blatant advertisement disguised as a press release.

Whether or not they run your story is always dependent on the news items of the week in question. However, if they decide not to run your article because of a more newsworthy story don't get upset. Simply ask them to hold it over. Give their readers the opportunity of a free sample by offering the paper some free sessions. This will sometimes be enough to ensure a space on the competition page, along with associated "free" publicity. Don't be afraid to ask them if they will let you have all the entries so that you can follow them up, including the losers.

Early November is a good time to send out press releases extolling the benefits of a life coach for the New Year, when most people focus on resolutions. You can also point out that a few life coaching sessions would make an original Christmas gift.

When you are at any gathering of people, you may be asked what you do for a living. Be sure to have an interesting answer ready. Here are a few suggestions that are bound to start a conversation:

- "I open the door of your potential"
- "I'm the deliverer of dreams"
- "I am your potential wizard"
- "I hold the key to success"
- "I unlock the doors of desires"
- "I'm a specialist in gap analysis – I close the gap between goals and achievement"
- "I'm in show business [you have probably heard this one before]: I show you how to achieve the life you want"

Follow this statement of interest immediately (without pausing) with a question: "May I ask you something? Is there any area in your life you wish you could change?" This will lead you on to explaining how you help your clients and how you can help them.

Be sure to present them with a business card and, as you hand it to them, repeat your interesting statement and tell them to call tomorrow when you can inspire them to achieve the change they said they wanted to make.

By far the most successful way of getting clients is by referrals from your existing clients. This can happen in either of two main ways. The first is that your client is so impressed that they tell their friends about you and pass on your telephone number. This really does happen. The second way is that you wait until the precise moment when a client excitedly tells you about how they have achieved one of their greatest dreams. Then, at that exact moment, you ask them if they know anybody who would like to share these wonderful feelings of success.

Agree what would be the best way forward. Would they be willing to tell this person about the service and give out your promotional material? Would they give you the name and telephone number of a friend they would like to enjoy the same level of success? Would they also help you both by telling their friend about their experiences with you?

The second approach is best because you get a recommendation *and* a telephone number so that you can call the prospective client. This keeps you in control and diminishes the opportunities for the prospective client to lose your number, forget to call you or not even bother to call. You should be the one to make this call as you are selling your services, which come highly recommended.

Whether you call the prospective client or they call you, you have to be able to provoke curiosity and then transform this call from an enquiry into a paying client. Quite often, your first opportunity to explain your service to a prospect client will be over the telephone.

There is a model that is easy to remember and easy to use. Although it cannot guarantee to transform prospects into paying clients, it gives you a framework to follow and makes sure that you do not forget any important stages in the process. It is called the RABIT model because it shows each of five vital stages clearly. It is easy to remember, and it can produce countless offspring in the form of clients.

R	**Recount** to your prospect a few of the benefits of life coaching.
A	**Ask** about the prospect.
B	Your **background**, qualifications, experiences, successes and fee.
I	**Interest** testing.
T	**Time** to close the deal and get the business.

Let us look at these in more detail.

R stands for **recounting** a few of the benefits of life coaching. Tell them briefly, about one of your great successes. If you do not have a success story yet, tell them a successful coaching story that you have heard about.

Make sure you know that you have decided beforehand which benefits you are going to talk about. After outlining each one, ask your prospect if this benefit would be of interest to them. Avoid long lists of benefits, as this actually detracts from the overall effect and can, in the worst scenario, sound like a sales pitch. This is not a sales pitch like a double-glazing or life-insurance sell. You want the prospect to become a client because they want to, not because you have done a hard sell on them.

A is for **asking** the prospect to tell you a bit about their background and what prompted them to enquire about life coaching. "Briefly, what is your current situation?" or, "If you were to hire me as your coach, what would you want to work on?"

When you have an answer, use metaphor (see Chapter Sixteen) to compare what they want to achieve with someone else you know who had a similar situation and how they overcame it with your help (or how it was overcome with the help of another life coach).

B is a little about your **background**. Include appropriate qualifications, experience, your successes and, if you have one, a reference from a satisfied client who is prepared to say how good you are. The purpose here is to attract a new paying client, not to bore the other person with your life history and achievements. To ensure you select the best examples of your background, make a list of all your achievements and qualifications.

You will find it useful to create your own Briefing Matrix. Once you have listed all your possible background items, ask yourself this. "If I were enquiring about life coaching, how would this information really make me want to hire this coach?"

Give each item on the list a mark between 1 and 10, where 1 is "not at all likely" and 10 is "very likely." Once you have a score in each box, add up the totals across the page. The three highest-scoring items are the ones to use.

The first example below receives only 11 marks. That is because, although it is important to the coach on a personal level, it is not a high selling point for life coaching. The next example scores highly because it shows how you helped your client to achieve a goal.

Prospective clients will be more impressed with your results rather than qualifications.

Briefing Matrix – the Benefits of using my Services

List	Essential to know	Nice to know	Fairly interesting	Really relevant	Totals
BA Hons Ancient Greek	5	3	2	1	11
Helped a client move from manager to director	10	10	10	10	40

Using these column headings, draw your own grid on a clean sheet of plain paper. At this stage there is no limit to the number of items on your first list, but remember that you are going to use only the three items with the highest scores.

Develop these three items into a simple, brief and positive sentence. Then ask a trusted colleague if they would hire you on this basis. Avoid asking a friend, as they may be tempted to protect your ego by telling you what they think you want to hear.

A reliable statement that I use at this stage in the model is, "I need to be convinced that you're committed to achieving results because I have a hundred per cent success rate currently and I won't take you on if you're not committed to working hard for change." Prospects usually affirm their commitment, and that gives you a good opening to go on to the cost of your services.

Move on to your fee structure and mention any special introductory offers. I suggest that you have at least three alternative pricing options. For example, you could have Platinum, Gold and Silver fees based on the length of each coaching session.

Platinum	4 calls of 1 hour's duration
Gold	4 calls of 45 minutes' duration
Silver	4 calls of 30 minutes' duration

This table is based on payment in advance for all four calls. Pricing will depend on the current marketplace. Research the Internet for coaching practices with pricing information and adapt to suit your experience and practice.

If the prospect states that they would like to meet you and you then have to travel for the meeting, be sure that the client knows that you will always charge travel time. After all, while you are travelling you could have been taking another fee-earning coaching call.

If you are nervous about asking for money, practise with your friends and family until you sound confident. It is very important that you sound sure of your pricing policy. If you are not confident, then your client will not feel confident in agreeing to pay you.

The I of RABIT is for **interest** testing. This simply means asking the prospect if they are interested in what they have heard so far. Phrase your questions to get a positive answer: "This is a really interesting and exciting way to shape your future, isn't it?"

As soon as they answer "Yes" proceed to the T which means it is **time** to pose the "close question." Here is the one that has yielded me the greatest number of clients.

"So, can you see [or feel, or whatever their preferred representational system is – see Chapter Eleven] any reason not to proceed?" Now remain silent until the prospect speaks. If your prospect says no, you move to the alternative close. This simply means that you offer two different dates and times for appointments and ask which one they prefer. It distracts them from the decision they have just made by offering another, easier decision. You are simply asking if they prefer Monday or Friday? This really does ease their decision-making process and helps things along. Do not worry about the ethics of the alternative close, because it works on only clients who want to go ahead and need a gentle push. The clients who do not want to use you will not fall for it.

We have almost completed the foundations for your professional life coaching practice. There is only the remaining issue of ethics or code of conduct.

At present, there is no governing body for life coaching and it is up to us as individuals to ensure that we do not bring this wonderful profession into disrepute. Think carefully about what you will and will not do, what principles and values you stand for and how you conduct yourself and your practice.

Then prepare a code-of-conduct or charter-of-business document. You can send this to new clients to let them know how you will work. Here is a copy of my own business charter as an example.

Charter of Life Coaching Practice

Aim

I aim to provide a high-quality professional coaching service, which serves the needs and interests of my clients. I aim to build long-term relationships with you. These, in turn, will enable us to work together to enhance your working and business skills and competencies. I aim to support you in achieving your goals, career, health, wealth, contribution, relationships and mission.

My Values

Respect, Integrity, Honesty, Quality, Professionalism, Partnerships and Value.

Guarantees

I will make every effort to supply the coaching hours contracted to high standards. Should I make a mistake I will seek to remedy it to your satisfaction.

Courtesy

In all dealings I will maintain a high level of courtesy to clients, their employees and their customers. I will reply promptly to all and any enquiries.

Information and Assistance

Within the limits of maintaining the confidentiality of other clients, I will provide all the information and assistance that I can, to fulfil any contracts to the highest standards.

Fairness

I will seek to be fair in all aspects of my business relationship with clients.

Confidentiality

I will at all times respect the confidentiality of clients and will not divulge any information unless required to by the law.

Time Allocation

At all times, I will allocate and be available for the session times agreed in the contract and remuneration will be apportioned in all circumstances for this allocation.

Do please ensure that you can fulfil all that you promise. Now you are ready to launch your professional coaching practice, although you will find more advanced help and information in Chapter Eighteen.

Summary

- This is probably the most important chapter of this book
- Prepare a code of conduct or charter of business practice
- Have an interesting introductory sentence to generate clients
- Use RABIT to generate offspring clients and convert prospects into clients

Chapter Seven

Coaching for Results

'You may get the ingredients and the recipe correct,
but the only true test of success is the finished result'

Synopsis

**Using the I-CAN-DO life coaching model will help you to grow
your practice and increase result attainment with your clients.
The life coaching chart or matrix will provide a framework for
you to coach each client. Charging for missed appointments is
part of marketing and image, not just loss of time. Should you
make notes during a life coaching session? Deal with a rapport
ruiner by using a pattern interrupt. Renewals are the most cost-
effective way to build your practice.**

Although life coaching has an approach that is personally
designed according to the needs of each client, there are several
models that can provide a sound foundation. You may like to think
of this as being similar to the motor manufacturing industry, where
a common framework and design can allow the public to choose
from a variety of models from the basic and practical box on
wheels to a sleek and sexy coupé.

One of the most useful coaching models is I-CAN-DO, which has
been adapted from several sources, including the GROW model by
John Whitmore. This is fully described in his book *Coaching for
Performance*.

INVESTIGATE
CURRENT
AIMS
NUMBER
DATE
OUTCOME

The I-CAN-DO life coaching model is flexible and easily adapted for applications focused on overall life aims or for setting and evaluating the outcomes of a session. The mnemonic is a perfect fit for the ideal mental approach that your clients should work towards.

At the outset, I tell my clients, I base my life coaching on the I-CAN-DO model. This sets the frame in a client's mind that the responsibility for the achievement and success comes from them rather than from me.

Here are some simple guidelines to its use and application. You tell your client that you will be using the model, explain that the letter I stands for **investigate**, and continue: "This means that I want you to investigate what is important to you and what you know about how I can help you. Spend some time before our first coaching session thinking about you. When this is done, send me an e-mail or drop me a line with your thoughts, your **current** situation briefly described, and state your overall **aims** in life. To guide your thoughts I will send you a chart. This covers the areas in your life that I want you to consider."

Life Coaching Chart

Topic	Current situation	Hours per 98-hour week	Future aims
Health What is important to you when you consider your health?			
Wealth What constitutes a wealthy life for you?			
Family What and who are important to you regarding your family?			

continued ...

Topic	Current situation	Hours per 98-hour week	Future aims
Relationships Who is important to you?				
Contribution How important is your contribution to the world?				
Spiritual What is important to you as far as spiritual growth is concerned?				
Career/job What is important to you in your work?				
Playtime What do you do just for fun?				
Lack What other areas in your life require attention?				

Explain that you need an honest and detailed account of the amount of time spent on the topics in a typical week. The 98-hour week allows for seven days, each of fourteen hours. You can be flexible if your client suggests a longer or shorter typical day, but do not be conned: each category must be completed. When you know the time spent in each area, you will have a perspective of client's priorities. The results often reveal serious deficits in one or more of areas, which indicates an unbalanced lifestyle. Once you have received the completed chart, you have finished the first three stages of the I-CAN-DO life coaching model (investigate, define current situation and identify aims.)

Let us now complete the I-CAN-DO mnemonic:

I: **Investigate** what is so important to the client that they decided to hire you?

C: What is their **current** life situation (use the Life Coaching Chart opposite)?

A: What are their **aims** in life?

N: What is the **number** of alternative ways of achieving the aims?

D: By what **date** do they want to achieve their aims?

O: What are the **outcome** achievement indicators?

The completion of the Life Coaching Chart allows time to prepare yourself for the first coaching call with sufficient information for you to make an impact for your clients. This approach is also a tremendous indicator of your client's commitment to life coaching. In life coaching terms, commitment is evident when the client continues to complete the task long after their initial mood – the one they had at the time they decided to do it with you – has left them.

If the client does not send you the completed chart before your first planned session, you must challenge this lack of response and commitment. There may be a valid reason for their not sending you the information, such as a death or tragedy in the family. However, if they do not have a valid reason for neglecting these first steps of the I-CAN-DO model, then you need to make a serious choice. Do you want this client?

In most circumstances I would refuse to work with this client and immediately issue a full refund. I would remind them of our first discussion (see Chapter Six) when I told them, "I need to be convinced that you're committed to achieving results because I have a hundred per cent success rate currently and I won't take you on if you're not committed to working hard for change."

This is why the RABIT model (see Chapter Six) works well. When you use it during the first contact call with a client, you can quote it confidently if the need arises. There is a huge risk in accepting a client who does not provide you with the first task. There is no risk to the client but your reputation will be negatively affected. Your morale, motivation and self-belief will also need constant boosting when you work with a client who lacks commitment.

You just might accept a client who has fallen at this first hurdle, but only where the circumstances are exceptional and the client demonstrates absolute remorse. Ask what were the reasons behind them not accomplishing this critically important task. Immediately after listening to the explanation from the client, terminate the telephone call, having explained that this is the standard procedure. Also, explain there is no refund for this session because you have allocated your time. Suggest they use the remainder of this particular call time in preparation for the next call by completing steps I, C and A of the model – as previously agreed – and then forwarding it to you.

It is important that the client understands that your time is valuable and that they will have to pay for time wasted. In reality, it has very little to do with the payment, although time allocated to one client is time not charged to another. Of course you need the material resources to grow your practice but here the principle is more to do with respect for your professional time.

Charging for missed or misused call time brings your practice in line with dentists, lawyers and all other professional services. Failing to charge diminishes your professional image and can set the precedent of disrespect from this client. Ignoring this expense and conduct is giving the client a green light to go ahead with the behaviour, which they will take as an indication that there will be no impact on them for not completing tasks or for missing any and all appointments with you.

It is essential that you be fully prepared for each coaching call and you should allocate about fifteen minutes for this, immediately before the call.

First, locate the client file. This is where you store all your information on this client. It may be a physical written file or an electronic computer file. Whichever format it takes, you must have taken into account the Data Protection Act (see Chapter Eighteen).

Study the file from the very first coaching session to the most recent and familiarise yourself completely with this client's background. Do not be tempted to limit your study to the last call because this will not fully prepare you for anything that may arise.

Clients often assume that you know a part of their personal history, even if they have never told you about it. Without a full review of all your notes, you will be unprepared to challenge this assumption. With a full review prior to the call you can confidently say to your client, "I'm sorry, Paul, but I'm confident you haven't spoken about this before. Please take a few minutes to get me up to speed on this topic." Or, "Paul, I remember all of our calls clearly and you haven't mentioned this aspect before. Please give me a brief summary so that I can help you in this area."

Make sure you have checked and arranged all your administration tools and they are close to hand. You should have with you:

- a pen or pencil
- a notepad or the client forms that you work with
- a telephone within easy reach and with a dial tone
- a drink of water handy
- your appointments diary

In addition, you should ensure that:

- You have been to the toilet. This may seem over the top, but I can assure you many life coaches have been caught short because they did not relieve themselves before taking a coaching call.
- Any reference material or books (names and addresses of professionals you are happy to recommend) or other resources that you may want to offer to your client are to hand. It sounds unprofessional if you are scrabbling around for contact details while in the middle of a coaching call.

So much for the administrative details. Now turn your attention to the critically important aspects of your personal preparation. What do you want to accomplish during this call? How can you best serve this client? Do you have any mental barriers relating to the potential of this client? What are your values and what is your philosophy for life coaching?

The singular most important question before you pick up the telephone is, "Am I in a peak state?" The answer to this question must be "yes."

If the answer is "no" or "not sure," you must do some rapid state-control work to change to your peak state. The conditions for outstanding life coaching sessions are completely reliant on this. In peak state you are feeling great, mentally alert and excited about the forthcoming coaching call. Anything less than this does you and the profession a disservice. Learn how to get into a peak state in a clock tick because that is all it takes for the phone to ring and a client to speak to you. Preparation is the key to life coaching success.

Some of these preparations start as soon as you have received the chart from your client. As you read their goals and aims you need to consider a *number* (The N of I-CAN-DO) of different methods, routes or ways that your client can take or make to secure a successful outcome. During the coaching call, ask your client if they can think of another way (from the original method they volunteered) to reach the aim or outcome. Guide them into giving you at least two or three alternative routes to a successful outcome, as this will open their eyes to flexibility. Flexibility is a fundamental skill needed by the client to increase their number of successfully achieved aims.

Health is one of the chart topics that I am very concerned with. Your client must have a commitment to being healthy by putting into place a carefully planned nutritious diet. I do not mean a slimming diet: I mean a diet in terms of a planned selection of food. They should also take some form of exercise.

It is your responsibility to encourage your clients to work on all aspects of their health. If you do not encourage and challenge your client to commit to a health regime, the *health* topic of the chart eventually becomes the *lack* topic. This can easily happen when clients neglect their health in the belief that they will always be fit. After all, this has been true so far in their lives. The problem is that it takes years of compounded maltreatment for their health eventually to break down. Usually when their health does break down, the results are fairly dramatic. So the lack of health presents a goal: that of the need to regain the health. It is your role as client guardian to prevent this breakdown.

Should a client say that they wish to do more (or some) exercise, you need to ask what they have in mind. If this client does not normally undertake any exercise, they will normally answer, "I should join a gym." On the surface this sounds like a great idea. However, there are two problems with this. The first is the use of the word "should." It is mostly used as a modal verb to mean "ought to" (see Chapters Thirteen and Fourteen) and indicates a lack of true commitment to the task. The second problem is that they are currently not a member of a gym and feel that joining one is the only option.

If a client proposes going to the gym as the option for becoming healthy, you must ask the following questions.

"Have you belonged to a gym before?" If the answer is yes, you need to find out why they stopped going and how much they enjoyed it before exploring alternatives. The best possible answer is, "I did enjoy going and look forward to going again." Unfortunately, this is not often the case. If the answer is no, that they have not joined a gym, then you must discover the reason behind the negative response. It will be a complete waste of your efforts to get your client to a fit state of health if they are resistant (in no matter how small a way) to attending a gym.

Here is where the **number** of alternatives in the I-CAN-DO model comes fully into force. You need to guide your client into looking at different ways of achieving fitness. A good question to ask is, "What other everyday things could you do to increase your level of fitness?"

You are seeking such answers as, " I could walk to work"; "I could use the stairs instead of the lift every time"; "I could park my car a couple of roads away from work and walk the distance every day"; "I could get off the bus one stop before my home and walk the rest of the way."

The key to attaining fitness is a daily change to routine both with diet and with exercise. If you can get your client to walk the stairs instead of taking the lift every day, their improvement will be steady and more permanent. Another tip is to encourage your client to discuss what forms of exercise they used to like doing or that they have done while on holiday (swimming, for instance, or dancing). If they mention that they swim on holiday, ask them if they could incorporate swimming once or twice a week into their routine. Listen for hesitation!

COACH: You said you liked swimming on holiday. What do you need to do in order for you to enjoy going for a swim locally?

CLIENT: I'm not sure.

COACH: Would going with a friend or colleague from work make swimming more enjoyable?

CLIENT: Mm, possibly. [This is a danger signal.]

COACH: On a scale of one to ten, ten being fully committed to becoming fit, where are you? [You need an eight or above for results.]

CLIENT: About a seven.

COACH: Do, *right now*, what you need to do to take your commitment to being healthy to a ten. [Wait quietly for a response. If you are dealing with an "away-from" client (see Chapter Fifteen, which deals with Meta-programs), rephrase this question as, "… your commitment to preventing a serious illness to a ten."]

CLIENT: Well, now you mention the reasons why I decided to consider my health, it's a ten.

COACH: So, on a scale of one to ten, how committed are you to becoming healthy?

CLIENT: Ten.

Coach: If your commitment to becoming healthy is a ten, what's your commitment to walking up the stairs instead of taking the lift?

CLIENT: Ten.

COACH: Are you absolutely sure, because I don't want to get to our next call to discover that you've taken the lift instead of walking?

CLIENT: Yes, I'm sure.

COACH: Great. Now, on the subject of swimming, how committed are you?

CLIENT: Well, er, about an eight.

COACH: How are you going to ensure that you go swimming once or twice a week?

CLIENT: Well, I don't really know.

COACH: If you did know, what would you do?

CLIENT: Well, I could join the aqua-aerobics class.

COACH: Why the aqua-aerobics class?

CLIENT: My friend Val goes to the class and she enjoys it. I could join her.

COACH: Would joining Val help you to keep to your commitment to increasing your fitness?

CLIENT: Yes, it would.

COACH: On a scale of one to ten, how committed are you to joining Val at the aqua-aerobics class?

CLIENT: Ten.

COACH: Ten. Are you sure?

CLIENT: Yes.

COACH: What do you need to do immediately after this conversation in order to ensure that you attend the next aqua-aerobics class?

CLIENT: I need to ring Val and arrange to go with her.

COACH: What time will you ring Val?

CLIENT: She works during the day, so I'll ring this evening.

COACH: Great. What time this evening?

CLIENT: Between six thirty and eight.

COACH: So, you're committed to ringing Val this evening between six thirty and eight to arrange to go with her to the aqua-aerobics class, yes?

CLIENT: Yes.

You will have noticed that the process seemed quiet repetitive and may appear to be patronising. You do need to take care not to patronise while also ensuring commitment to tasks that your client has spent years avoiding.

Apply repetition until you are absolutely sure that the client is going to do the task. As soon as you are convinced, you must summarise the task and the commitment. Some clients are committed from the beginning and you do not need to use the one-to-ten commitment scale. One of my clients used her sessions to tell me what she had done and what she intended doing before the next session. My input was very little; she needed only the structure of a reporting system to impel her into action.

When you have reached agreement with your client on which tasks are going to be done and by which method or route, they have to appoint a realistic **date** by which the task will be finished (the D of I-CAN-DO). Listen very carefully for the tone of commitment to the proffered date. Clients often indicate, by their voice tone, a lack of commitment to a task when they feel trapped into deciding a time for completion.

When your client consults their diary or, if they respond confidently and quickly with a date, then you can be almost sure that the task will be done within the time. However, if there is hesitation, you can be just as sure that the task will not be completed when agreed. It is all in the tone of voice, so listen very carefully.

If you detect that your client does not sound completely convincing during the date part of the I-CAN-DO model, you can once again use a questioning-and-refining process along the lines of, "How committed are you to hitting this target date on a scale of one to ten?"

Finally, you need to distinguish how your client will know that their **outcome** (the O of the model) has been successfully reached. This is where we meet the outcome achievement indicators I mentioned above.

Ask, "What would success look like with this outcome? What evidence do you need to show this outcome has been achieved?" Or you could say, "Describe exactly how you will know that you have triumphantly reached your outcome."

This step is critical for both you and your client. It is easy to assume that you both know what success looks like. Then you can be astonished when it is not reached, simply because you had a different concept of what success meant. Always ask your client for outcome indicators, as it provides you and them with exact measurements on results.

In Chapter Eleven we will meet what are known as client representational systems. It is important to ask your client to describe the outcome indicators in their preferred representational system. Briefly, clients predominantly use one of the following three senses: visual, auditory and kinaesthetic (the perception of motion, position and weight of the body). Clients will clearly and precisely describe their outcome indicator when they are asked to do so using the language of their preferred representational system.

For example, if a coach asks a visual client to describe the outcome indicators using words connected with the sense of sight, the conversation could proceed like this.

COACH: What will this outcome *look* like when you've attained success?
CLIENT: I'd be wearing a bright-red suit with matching accessories. My black zipper briefcase would be in my right hand. The grass would be very green, the sky blue and everyone would be looking very happy and smiling at me.

If a coach uses "visual" words, this makes it easy for the visual client to describe their mental vision in great detail. Now, if a coach was to ask an auditory client for outcome indicators using "auditory" words, the conversation could sound like this.

COACH: *Tell* me, what will this outcome be like when you've attained success?
CLIENT: I would want to sing about it and shout from the rooftops. Everyone would be saying how happy they were for me and congratulating me on my success.

Notice the difference: the situation is the same but the client experiences it very differently. Finally, the kinaesthetic-client scenario.

COACH: What will it *feel* like when you've reached the outcome?
CLIENT: It would feel wonderful. I'd be strong, proud and full of courage and everyone would be patting me on the back and shaking my hand.

Using the client's preferred representational system at this stage in the I-CAN-DO model really makes the difference for both of you. Clients will give you a very clear, sound and solid measure for determining their own outcome indicators. Beware that the converse can present problems for the coach and client. If you do not speak in your client's representational language pattern you make it harder for them to understand what you want.

Misunderstandings occur and outcomes are confused. Spend time studying Chapter Eleven, which will help you to conduct effective coaching sessions with your clients.

The I-CAN-DO model of life coaching should be used on each individual aim or goal that your client presents. All the areas of the matrix – health, wealth, family, relationships, contribution to the world, spiritual, career, leisure and lack – should be processed through the model. If, for example, a client under the health aim wants to lose some weight.

> **I**: What is your reason for wanting to lose some weight? (Investigate)
> **C**: What is your current weight? (Current)
> **A**: Exactly what weight do you want to be? (Aims)
> **N**: What are the successful methods of weight loss you have heard about or experienced? (Number)
> **D**: By what date do you want to be your ideal weight? (Date)
> **O**: How will you know you have succeeded? (Outcome)

The temptation on the outcome indicator is to assume that the scales will be the measure of success – and in most cases they will. However, clients are known to have answered this final question in many different ways. One of my male clients said he would know he had reached the ideal weight when his dinner jacket fitted him again. Interestingly, he had given me an ideal weight goal in kilograms but when he said he had reached the goal he judged success only by whether the jacket fitted. He did not use the scales to measure his goal achievement, nor did I ask him to do so. The reason I did not pursue his use of scales was because, during our conversations, he clearly revealed that he was not interested in actual body weight but only interested in fitting into his old jacket.

Use the model on each client goal and keep a note of what is discussed. Many life coaches and life-coach trainers have rigorously discussed making notes during a life coaching session. The argument for not taking notes during the coaching session is that the coach will thus be allowed absolute focused attention on the client, to be there, experiencing and attending to the client fully. If the coach is busy making notes during the session the client is not getting undivided attention.

One excellent life coaching trainer, Sangeeta Mayne of L.I.F.T. International, says, "It is really important to stay in the moment, be present and really connected with your client in order to fully understand their experience." By being completely focused on your client and living in the moment you will be able to recall the experience fully in order to make any necessary notes at the end of the session. This method offers the coach and the client a spiritual experience, which grows and develops during the relationship.

The downside to leaving the note taking until after the session has finished is that the process uses extra time and the coach needs to allow for this during the appointment scheduling. Therefore, a client session will include the preparation time (usually about 15 minutes), the actual coaching-session time (30 to 60 minutes) and note-making time (depending on detail, 10 to 20 minutes). The longest time for one client would be somewhere around 100 minutes. The important thing is not the amount of time spent but the amount of time charged for. If you believe that you should be fully present and in the moment with your clients you need to charge accordingly. All time spent on a client, directly or indirectly, should be charged unless you are coaching for a charity, coaching children or have specially agreed circumstances and arrangements.

Charging in this way may be difficult when you are first starting your practice and you may choose not to charge for the time spent outside of direct contact. Remember that you can change your method of charging at any time, as long as you give your client advance warning. The best time to introduce a new charge scale is at the end of a series of coaching sessions. So, if a client has purchased twelve sessions on a renewable basis, you can advise them, during the eleventh session, that the basis is changing. This gives your client warning and sufficient time to decide whether to continue with you.

You will lose some clients when introducing a fee increase, but you can reduce the impact by broaching the subject in a positive way. Start by reminding your client about the successes that they have achieved during the partnership with you. Then briefly explain your new pricing structure, followed swiftly by refocusing on their outcomes or goals.

Use their Meta-program (see Chapter Fifteen) to help you. For example, if your client is *towards* goals, they like to achieve, attain and prioritise. Remind them of their achievements and the exciting new goals yet to be attained. Get them to imagine what it will be like when they have reached their new goals.

Away-from clients recognise what should be avoided. They want to get away from a problematic situation. Motivate them by emphasising what they have left behind since your partnership and ask them what it would be like to remain in their current situation, rather than move away from it.

The opposing argument for note taking during the coaching session is just as valid. If you take notes as you are going along you have an instant record of the coaching session. You know what was agreed and when it will be accomplished. The agreed tasks can be easily recalled by looking at your notes at the end of the session.

Another advantage of taking notes during the session is that you save the note-making time after the call and this can be used for further coaching sessions. The disadvantage is that taking notes requires some of your attention and this is therefore not focused fully on your client. Some clients will automatically feel the distraction and be unsettled by note taking. Other clients will be perturbed if you are *not* making notes throughout the conversation, as they will feel that you are not listening.

You must decide which works better for you. There are no rules stating that you must use only one method to the exclusion of the other. This means that you can take notes with some clients and not with others. If you are going to make notes during the coaching sessions, it is recommended that you ask your client: "I'd like to make notes as we go along to ensure that I remember all your important goals and aims, as I don't want to miss anything. Is it all right with you that I make notes as we discuss points?" They will have the opportunity of expressing their feelings and you will both get off to a good start. If you take your notes electronically ensure that all the sounds have been removed and that you have full agreement to take notes in this manner from your client. Some clients are offended by the sound of clacking keyboards and associate the sound with poor customer service. This is possibly because of a bad previous anchoring experience (see Chapter Ten) with a monolithic customer-service department of a large corporation.

At the end of the coaching session, after you have completed the I-CAN-DO model against all the topics on the chart or matrix, you must summarise the agreed tasks. Some coaches like to tell their clients what tasks they believe have been agreed upon with their dates for achievement. The advantage of this method is that the client is made emphatically aware that you were paying attention to them and you know what has to be accomplished. The disadvantage is the unlikely event that you may forget one or two of the agreed tasks. If this occurs you are in trouble and you will have lost your client's confidence. One way of overcoming this potential disaster is to be honest and say why you missed the tasks out. The reason could be as simple as that the two tasks were on the other side of the page and you did not turn it over.

The preferred approach to use during the summary part of the coaching call is to ask your client to tell you what they believe they have agreed to do. Then, as they are telling you what they agreed, you can confidently confirm each point. An added advantage of this approach is that, when a client has forgotten one or two of the tasks (generally the ones they were not too keen on doing), you can remind them. This sends a very strong message that you were fully attentive to the client throughout the session and that you will not let them get away with anything.

It can be a good time to bring some humour to the call and lighten the experience for the client. If you think your client would enjoy being teased you could say, "Aha! You thought you could pull the wool over my eyes, did you?" Or, "You thought I'd forget that one, didn't you? Well no chance of that." Remember, you and your clients need to enjoy the coaching experience and a little humour goes a long way.

Now that we have reached it, we need to explore the topic of humour. It is a tricky servant and will trip you up if you do not take everything into account. Some clients would find great fun in a joke about mothers-in-law, while others would be absolutely horrified. Some clients would consider a comment about their not achieving a task – a remark such as "You slippery eel!" – to be funny and endearing, while others would take great umbrage. It is often the little observations, said in jest with an endearing intention, that cause the big problems. The little witticisms that we banter with our friends and our business colleagues are easily quoted in an unguarded moment with a client. If you are fully engaged and congruent with a client, this is unlikely to occur. However, it does happen, so you need to be alert to signals about what is acceptable with each client if your coaching style includes humour or banter.

A recent area for concern is the e-mail joke. It is a trendy and virulent pastime of World Wide Web surfers to send jokes by e-mail. Never send e-mail jokes to a client, even if you are absolutely sure that they will find it really funny. The trouble with e-mail jokes is that you are not there when the e-mail is opened and have no control over the state that your client is in at that time. Think about this for a moment. You have sent a very funny joke, via the e-mail, about an undertaker who loses a corpse. You know your client really well and are absolutely sure they would find the joke hysterically funny. What you do not know is that today their father died in a car crash. The joke is now not at all funny.

As a rule of thumb, never send jokes of any kind over the Internet. Limit light humour during sessions with clients when you have a really strong relationship. This would generally mean the client has been with you for two full programmes (24 coaching sessions) and you are fully aware that the risk you are taking by being humorous can be offset by the great achievements you have made with your client. Avoid humour and jokes with new clients.

During the coaching process there may be times you feel worried that you do not know what to say. This is more likely to occur during your early stages of life coaching. Do not worry. If you are coaching from a genuine desire to help your client, this will never happen. However, to put your mind at rest, if you do ever hit a blank, always fall back on trusty questions. One really effective question is, "What advice would you give yourself if you were the coach?" Clients always have the resources within to answer this question. Fear that a client may come back with "You're the coach, not me!" can sometimes prevent us from asking this valuable question. Overcome this retort with, "Yes, I am your coach, and my experience tells me that clients usually know what is the best route for themselves but are afraid to speak it for fear of failure or fear of success. So, what would your advice be?" Another way of putting this is, "Yes, I'm happy to be your coach. My experience tells me that clients in the same situation as you are currently facing usually have the answer but are afraid to speak it for fear of failure or fear of success. So, what would your advice be?"

Another useful question to ask is, "If you could go back ten years and had the opportunity to coach yourself, what would you have said?" The trick here is to give your clients time to answer. They will need time to consider and reflect in order to produce a suitable response. Wait quietly and patiently for their reply. If they become stuck gently nudge them by offering this: "If not you, what advice would [a fortune teller, wizard, prophet, mentor, wise master] have given you?" Clients will come up with extraordinarily insightful responses, which will amaze and enthral you. The greatest gift of being a life coach is that you get to be coached yourself during these golden moments.

I sometimes use hypnotic language to encourage clients to come up with the answers they need. "Imagine for a moment that you have a friend who knows you inside out – what advice would they give you?" After the client has told you the advice the imaginary friend would give, you need to follow up with these questions: "So is this good advice?" and "Will this advice help you towards your outcome?"

An auspicious question for many situations is, "If there's one thing you would have done differently, what would it have been?" This question often gives your client insights that they have not previously considered. Once more, it is vital to give your client time to respond, as time usually furnishes remarkable results. The advantage of this question is that it works with life goals and equally as well with small tasks that were not successfully achieved.

The underlying skills of outstanding coaching sessions are asking the right questions and emphatic listening to the responses. Within the chapters on language patterns you will find valuable questions to assist you as you grow and develop as a life coach.

There are occasions when a client becomes really stuck and I fall back on the I-CAN-DO life coaching model, using it as an incantation – I-Can-tation.

I encourage my clients to chant "I can do," whenever they have the need for resources or the desire for motivation. It is best to explain that incantations can be used positively or to destroy confidence. Clients are familiar with incantations: they use them all the time. You will often hear a client saying, "I can't do that." And they believe the chant they have just spoken.

Chanting is very powerful – you have only to watch the All Blacks rugby team prior to a game to see how powerful chanting can be. The enigma here is that we all chant every day – and usually several times a day – but the chants are "I can't" chants, not "I can" chants. Life coaching transforms negative chants into positive affirmations. This enables clients to reach goals they never dreamed they could reach.

Occasionally, a client will come to you presenting a serious life problem and it is your job to support them through this emotional period. Life coaching is about change and, if you are a good coach, you will aid and assist clients to change in many different ways and in all areas of life. Sometimes the client becomes almost unrecognisable to their family or friends and this can cause huge problems.

The family or friends could feel threatened by the changes in your client and this can be the source of much anxiety, anguish and arguments. Understand that your client changes *because they want to change* and that, at all times, your client chooses the responses they make. Do not become involved, other than in a coaching way, with domestic or friendship disputes. Never recommend divorce. Always coach for reconciliation and, if reconciliation fails, you have a clear conscience to support your client through any troubles that present themselves.

There have been marriage breakdowns, divorces and loss of friendships during life coaching programmes. These life problems are predictable when clients are changing into successful, confident people. Clients will evolve as they achieve more and more mastery of their own destiny. The evolution process will change the status quo within existing relationships and the relationships will flourish or wither.

If this happens to one of your clients, do not feel guilty (a natural reaction). Remember that your client has chosen to behave in such a way as to bring about the breakdown, not you. Your role is to support your client to achieve goals. Clients going through these types of change need slightly more sensitive management and encouragement.

A useful question for just this sort of dilemma is, "Have you overcome difficulties in the past?" Follow with, "What were the strengths that you called upon that helped you to get through that time? Were there any other strengths that you used?"

Coach to draw out as many different strengths as your client can recall and offer any that you think may have been used but overlooked. During one particularly testing coaching session I asked a client to go away and immediately write a list of all the good things he had done in his life. I told him to write down everything, large and small, including donations to charity, feeding a neighbour's cat or picking up someone's mail. He rang back the following day a confident and adjusted client, ready to tackle his goals. As clients rush around in their busy lives they can become overwhelmed by others' success and forget their own qualities. Remind clients how good they are at being the good person they are by suggesting they carry out this exercise in self-appreciation.

There are two more questions that you might consider using during the I-CAN-DO life coaching model. "Is doing [X] morally fair to all concerned?" and "Will doing this task take you closer to or further away from the major outcomes in your life?" The first question is valuable when a client is thinking of making a major career or lifestyle change. It transforms the focus from within the client to the external impact of the changes. From navel gazing to star gazing. A long silence following the first question may indicate some internal struggle. A sharp intake of breath is a good indicator that your client had not considered the full consequences of his or her choices. You will be glad you asked the question.

The second is a barometer question and should be used when you can clearly see that your client is going away from the original goals or aims and you want to refocus the energy. If you allow clients to go off on tangents you are taking the energy from the main outcome. This will have the impact of elongating the time span for accomplishing the overall outcome and will lessen the power of life coaching. Your client will not be truly passionate about the beneficial effects. It could also have an impact on your referral system, which was discussed in Chapter Six.

Occasionally you will have the wonderful experience of a rapport ruiner. Developing flexibility for dealing with a rapport ruiner is a communication technique that will serve you well for all situations where you encounter them. I called it a wonderful experience, because it allows you to practise your flexibility as a life coach and at the same time it tests your ability to control a judgmental disposition, should you possess such a thing. What is a rapport ruiner? Well, have you ever come into contact with a person who, if you said white, would say black; if you said go, would say stop? That is a rapport ruiner. They cannot help themselves, for they are compelled to respond in a contrary manner. Usually these behaviours will test most life coaches' flexibility to its limits and beyond.

Interestingly, the rapport ruiner does not consider him- or herself as being negative in approach, but most of the recipients of this behaviour would consider it negative. You will be able to detect a rapport ruiner during their first contact with you either face to face or over the telephone.

If you tell a rapport ruiner how life coaching can help them to achieve their goals, they are likely to respond with the fact that you could not possibly do that until you knew what their goals were. It is a waste of energy and time trying to rationalise with a rapport ruiner, so use this contact opportunity as a personal development experience for yourself. Take up the challenge and practise your state control (see Chapter Ten), your linguistic skills (see Chapters Thirteen and Fourteen) and your rapport skills (see Chapter Twelve). To help you deal effectively with a rapport ruiner there is a great linguistic trick. This actually brings you into rapport with the rapport ruiner by breaking their behaviour pattern, giving you a chance for positive communication.

Before I reveal the trick you must prepare yourself. Open your mind and promise that you will not unfairly judge what I am going to recommend. Also make a pledge that you will use the technique at least three times before you pass your verdict. It is a linguistic pattern and therefore needs fluency when using the phrase to a rapport ruiner. Consider the method of learning this trick as exactly the same method for learning a foreign language: you would repeat phrases several times before you spoke the foreign language, and so you must do the same with this phase.

During a normal coaching session with a rapport ruiner you might suggest:

COACH: Have you considered going to your manager?
RAPPORT RUINER: No. It wouldn't work anyway.
COACH: What about going to Human Resources?
RAPPORT RUINER: No. They wouldn't do anything if I did go to them.

It is quite probable that a coaching session with a rapport ruiner would continue along these lines and you would feel frustrated dealing with the continuous resistance. The trick is a linguistic pattern changer and the pattern needs to contain at least three negatives to be effective. For a non-rapport-ruiner the sentence will not make sense, nor will it sound pleasing. The important point is that it works, and that is all we need:

COACH : No. You wouldn't want to go to your manager, would you not?
RAPPORT RUINER: Yes, I would.

The rapport ruiner's compulsion to be contrary will get you a positive response. This linguistic pattern changer really works. The hurdle for you is making a sentence with three negatives sound fluent. That is where the practice is important. Remember, any sentences that you construct to combat the rapport ruiner's impact must have at least three negatives.

Renewals

In Chapter Six we looked at how to build a coaching practice, but we also need to consider how to keep a practice ongoing and profitable. Renewals and referrals are the mainstay of the life coaching practice, and without them there would be no practice and no profit. Referrals have already been extensively covered in Chapter Six.

Renewals need careful planning and preparation. You should not consider renewals as a separate entity to the individual coaching sessions. Renewals are harder to achieve if you leave the work until the last session of a life coaching programme.

Putting all your efforts into persuading the client to renew during the final session can cause you enormous pressure and is often unsuccessful. If you continuously provide an excellent service throughout the entire life coaching programme for each client, there is a much greater possibility your clients will renew with you. To increase the chances of their renewing, ask yourself this question during each session, "If this client had to decide right now whether to continue or renew their coaching programme with me, would they do so?" The answer should always be a convincing yes. If you are unsure that this client would renew, you will need to perform a detailed evaluation of the coaching session in doubt.

Questions you could to ask:

- What needs to be improved for this client to want to renew with me?
- Was I in a peak state throughout the entire life coaching session?
- How did I listen?
- Did I allow myself to become distracted at any time while I was engaged during the session?
- Did I miss any nonverbal clues?
- Did I assume, delete or distort information from this client?
- How judgmental was I?
- What needs to be improved for the next session?
- Are there any actions I can take between now and the next coaching session to improve my service to this client?

Concentrate on providing an outstanding service to your clients at each and every life coaching session and the renewals will follow automatically.

Renewal clients are the most profitable because all the costs of marketing and winning their business have already been accounted for during the sale of the first coaching programme. Renewal contracts are almost pure profit. You do not have to finance further marketing, further sales presentations or free coaching sessions. The costs of renewal may involve only the reissuing of contracts (if you originally chose to issue contracts), the cost of minimal stationery and the downloading of e-mails. There do not have to be any other costs involved.

It is in your financial interest to renew all life coaching programmes and here lies the dilemma: the most cost-effective way to run your practice is to renew all contracts with your clients; yet it is ethical to terminate a contract with a client as soon as you have completed the original goals. The question you have to ask yourself is, "Did I manipulate my client into renewal or did my client renew because of the outstanding service I provided?"

Be careful not to manipulate to gain renewals because you do not want clients with subsequent regrets. They will not recommend you to other people and they will be extraordinarily demanding throughout the life coaching programme. If you accidentally manipulate a client and you think they may be suffering renewal regrets, confront the problem by asking your client directly if this is the situation. Issue an immediate refund with a thank-you-for-your-patronage card. If you bury your head in the sand and continue regardless, you will pay a hidden cost for this action in the future.

Summary

- Use a coaching model
- Life coaching is about all areas of your client's life
- Use humour appropriately
- Referrals and renewals are critical to your success
- Renewals: the dilemma

Chapter Eight

The History and Development of Neuro-Linguistic Programming

'NLP – a minestrone soup of techniques for change'

Synopsis

Neuro-Linguistic Programming (NLP) was developed in the 1970s by John Grinder and Richard Bandler. It is the art and science of personal excellence. All life coaches should take personal responsibility for acquiring a sound knowledge of NLP basics.

At its simplest level, Neuro-Linguistic Programming is a series of techniques and procedures for coding human behaviour to assist the understanding of what people do and how they do it when they perform with excellence.

NLP was identified and developed in the early 1970s in the USA by John Grinder and Richard Bandler. Their work was based on studies and observations of excellent communicators, and their initial studies examined three famous therapists, Virginia Satir, Milton H. Erickson and Fritz Perls.

NLP is both an art and a science because everyone brings a unique style and a unique personality to whatever it is that they do. Art is how coaches make NLP special to them. Science lies in the methods and processes for discovering patterns used by excellent or outstanding individuals in their field of work to achieve exceptional results.

One of the keys to scientific methodology and process is that any given theory should be capable of being proven, replicated and modelled. In NLP, the modelling is based on the patterns, skills and techniques being used in counselling, education and business. These processes provide excellent aids for communication, personal development and accelerated techniques in therapy and learning. They work by providing a means of programming given responses to selected situations in order to deliver predictable outcomes or results.

If you are a coach, an appreciation of the history and evolution of NLP will help your understanding of its key features and their application. It is a short history and in this chapter, as an introductory taster, it has been made even shorter.

In 1972, Richard Bandler was a psychology student at the University of California, Santa Cruz. He had a particular interest in psychotherapy. John Grinder was an assistant professor of linguistics at the same university.

They worked together in studies of the astounding results being obtained by the top hypnotherapist Milton H. Erickson, family relationship solutions achieved by the family therapist Virginia Satir and the impact made by Fritz Perls, who was a psychotherapist and the originator of the therapy known as Gestalt.

Their studies led them to analyse the common points of success, to code them into patterns and then to model them. They recorded their findings in four books published between 1975 and 1977. These were *The Structure of Magic* (Parts 1 and 2) and *Patterns* (Parts 1 and 2).

Grinder and Bandler were also in contact with Gregory Bateson, a British anthropologist. Bateson had written on many different topics, including psychotherapy. He was best known for his Double Bind therapy in schizophrenia, an angle that had a profound effect on the original basis of NLP.

If Bandler and Grinder had foreseen the subsequent popularity of their findings, they might well have chosen a more marketable name. But they simply sought a descriptive title to cover the key aspects of their process of patterns of excellence in any field and the use of these as effective ways of thinking and communicating.

"Neuro" refers to the neurological processes of the body – the senses of taste, touch, smell, sound and vision. "Linguistic" refers to language. There are two predominant language models in NLP: the "Meta-Model" and the "Milton Model." "Programming" refers to the arrangement of ideas and the actions that this creates to produce results.

And so the name Neuro-Linguistic Programming was devised. Within a very short period it was being referred to by the easier-to-say abbreviation, NLP.

The nature of NLP means that it will always continue to grow and to generate new ideas, new techniques and new therapies. Indeed, as recently as 2000, John Grinder reaffirmed that it was always his earliest intention that his work should be seen as a beginning upon which others would build as they applied the principles to their own disciplines.

Not all life coaches will become NLP practitioners or masters, nor is there any need for them to do so. Not all NLP practitioners and masters will have the desire or skills to become life coaches. However, every truly effective life coach will have a sound understanding and awareness of basic NLP and they will quickly appreciate how powerful it can be as a tool to help their clients move towards their desired results, outcomes or objectives. This section of the book introduces some of these techniques from the life coaching perspective. Further reading on NLP is strongly recommended for every coach.

Most NLP textbooks suggest fourteen preconditions or presuppositions for students. Within the coaching situation, life coaches can reduce these to nine.

- You should have respect for the other person's model of the world.
- The meaning of communication is the response that you get.
- The mind and body affect each other, therefore if you think negatively you will get negative results and if you think positively you will get positive results.
- The words we use are not the event or the item that they represent.

- The most important information about a person is their behaviour, so, whatever behaviour is in a given situation, it is the best choice available.
- A person's behaviour is not who they are.
- People have all the resources and abilities that they need inside them to succeed.
- There is no failure, only feedback.
- If what you are doing is not working do something different. If we always do what we have always done, we will always get what we have always got. The only person who can change is you.

Summary

- NLP is a method of coding and understanding successful behaviour
- The resultant patterns allow the results to be replicated by modelling
- NLP is a constantly evolving and developing process
- There is no failure

Section 2

Advanced Life Coaching Skills

Chapter Nine

Reframes

*'When you set the frame you add to the picture.
When you reframe, you can totally change the picture'*

Synopsis

Once you have the understanding and flexibility of being able to frame and reframe you will understand why some clients were resistant to suggestions or hesitant in employing your services. Conversations will be clearer and you will get some quick results. When using framing with your clients, your recommendations will be more readily accepted. The main aim of a reframe is to help your client to see gains or benefits of any situation that they previously had not considered. Your role is to match the alternative reframe to the outcomes of each individual client.

When a painting is framed it is not changed. But the way the colours and shapes are strengthened or lessened can be dramatically altered and thus affect the interpretation intended by the artist.

The frame can make the painting more appealing, more exciting, dull and lacklustre, or simply not worth mentioning. Artists have been known to spend weeks or even years choosing the perfect frame for their work. Framing is so important that they sometimes experiment by putting several different frames around the painting until they find the ideal one. The frame is uniquely suited to the picture and harmoniously enhances every fine quality and potential of the creative work.

So what has all this talk about artists, paintings and frames to do with life coaching? The ability to listen to a story and then select the perfect frame for it is a precious skill. Life coaching does not require that you have this skill. You can work without it. However, once you have the understanding and flexibility to frame and reframe, you will then understand why some clients resisted your suggestions or were hesitant about employing your services. You will see how to make life more tranquil for yourself and your clients. Conversations will be clearer and you will achieve results without having to exert extra energy and enthusiasm into ideas. When you use framing, your clients more readily accept your suggestions, and resistance diminishes.

Framing skill is easily learned and you can have fun practising with everyone you meet. This means that once you start to use frames you will rapidly become adept at the skill with little effort from you.

The above paragraph is an example of a frame. I have applied the experience of learning a new skill to the frame of ease, speed of accomplishment and fun. I could just as easily have framed the skill with pain and hardship – like this: "Framing skill is difficult to learn and you must practise continuously with everyone you meet. This means that once you start to use frames you will gradually become adept at the skill with some effort from you."

You can frame carefully to get the results that you want. You can frame accidentally and jeopardise your results. Or you can do nothing. If you choose the second and third options you are choosing to make life coaching more arduous and less enjoyable for yourself.

One of the challenges faced by all coaches is to keep clients within the allocated time slot. It is very easy to overrun on time. This sets a poor precedent that will also reduce your profits. Frames offer excellent tools for dealing with this situation.

"Good morning, Jack. Before we start, I'd just like to confirm that this is a forty-five-minute session and it will finish at eleven forty-five. Is that so?"

This frame sets the time boundaries of the call and therefore, when forty minutes have elapsed, you can say at an appropriate break in conversation, "It's now eleven forty and we have only five minutes. What would be the most effective use of this time for you?"

The frame at the beginning of the call gives you the freedom to mention time at the end of the call without its becoming an embarrassing interruption. With this technique it simply becomes an anticipated completion of what was started. You brought the client's attention to the time at the outset of the session and did so again at the end to create a perfectly-rounded session. Using this type of framing in my own practice has helped to overcome the early difficulties of overrunning and its impact on the day's schedule.

The skill of reframing differs from framing because it gives your clients options that allow room for them to change their minds about events or beliefs. When you reframe an event for a client, you are not altering the events: all you are doing is looking at them in a different way. Whereas framing is *setting* the scene, reframing is *changing* the scene, by offering your clients an alternative frame. In this way you release them from being stuck with the same interpretation of the scene, picture or event.

Reframing is a brilliant tool for allowing you to help your clients to escape from being 'stuck in a rut of thinking.' You may be familiar with the well-used saying, "Is the cup half empty or half full?" Reframing allows you to move your client from seeing a half-empty cup to seeing one that is half full.

It is essential that you can spot the difference between clients' negative and positive thinking patterns. It is far more laborious working on goals with negative thinking patterns than it is on those with positive patterns. Reframing comes into its own here.

My first memory of reframing concerns a school prizegiving. I was with my friend, who was complaining that her mother and father were embarrassing. She said that she just wanted the ground to open and swallow her up. Apparently, they were showing her up because they were telling everyone what a clever daughter they had and how proud they were of her. My response was, "You're so very lucky to have a mum and dad who care enough about you to turn up. Neither of my parents bothered – do you want to swap parents?" My memory is not completely reliable but I would swear that she visibly perked up following our discussion and I do recall that, shortly after, she went and sat with her parents. Little did I realise then that this ability to reframe would become one of the most treasured of my skills as a life coach.

A client said that she thought her boss picked on her. I used a reframe by saying, "Yes, I can see how you could think your boss is picking on you. I have another client much like you – in fact in almost identical circumstances. She believes that she's very special and that her boss thinks she has special talents that deserve developing. The boss, although not a pleasant man with a brusque approach, is helping her to develop these talents and make her a more marketable person."

Always pause after a reframe to allow your client time to think about what you have said and to compare it with their own situation. In this example the client accepted the comparison and willingly spotted the "half-full cup." Clients have also rebuffed this reframe on occasions.

If a client does not accept the reframe you offer in this type of situation, they might have put a value on being a martyr. Depending on your relationship with this client, ask what benefits they are getting from maintaining this interpretation of the boss's behaviour. This option can be used only when your client–coach relationship is strong and your client has previously agreed that you can challenge their responses in order to help them.

When a reframe does not work you need to consider the background, previous history, goals and aims of the client. For example, if this client has previously mentioned that they want to go for promotion and indicated that they would be open to changing their job, you could select a different type of reframe.

"Several years ago I had a boss who used to pick on me and he made my life *miserable* [use your client's description here], but one day I decided that I would use this as an inspiration to go and find the promotion I deserved. It took me quite some time before I found the job I wanted, but the fact that I'd decided to leave gave me a greater sense of purpose. And do you know what happened? By the time I was due to leave that company my relationship with my boss had changed, so I decided to stay and develop my career within a company structure I was already familiar with."

Using this type of reframe gives your client flexibility to stay or to leave with the added implication that they must do something. It offers alternative choices of career direction. Also, the reframe suggests that they are in control of how they interpret their boss's behaviour and, if they change the meaning, they change the results.

While talking about the benefits of exercise to one of my clients, she responded, "I'm not keen on exercise because I don't like being sweaty." She was a regional sales manager for a large computer company and I had already discovered that she put immense value on the quality of her skin, drinking only water and freshly-squeezed juices. She also felt constantly stressed with the pressure of her position. Armed with this information, I composed my reply along these lines:

"That's interesting. I used to feel the same about sweating until a beauty therapist explained that when you sweat, particularly during exercising, you're not only creating a beautiful body but, more importantly, you're purifying the skin in the most natural and effective way possible. Apparently, when you exercise you produce endorphins, which travel around your body destressing your cells, and the sweating process expels the ageing oxidants keeping your skin young, clean and healthy."

She joined a health club with a sauna and combined swimming with a short spell in the sauna. It was not quite the result I had in mind – I wanted her to take up an aerobic type of exercise – but the overall result was an exercise regime and therefore she had started on a course of action she had been putting off for several years. To my knowledge she still swims regularly.

There are two significant points in this example. The first is that the reframe encouraged her to explore the possibility of exercise; and the second, for the life coach, is that it is about the client's outcomes. The main aim of a reframe is to help your client to see the gains or benefits of a situation. Your role is to match the alternative reframe to the outcomes of each individual client. In this way your clients will be willing to consider or accept the new ideas.

One of my clients was angry with his partner and complained that she was always tidying up around him and behind him. When dealing with clients of the opposite sex I always use a male third-party example. This eliminates the possibilities of clients justifying nonacceptance on the basis of, "Well, that's how women see things."

The response I used was, "A doctor was telling me about his wife's need to show him how much she loved him by constantly tidying up after him. It used to really annoy him until he understood that, by allowing her to demonstrate her love in this way, he was appreciating her contribution to the marriage. He also realised that he had some habits that irritated her but she accepted these as part of the whole person with whom she had fallen in love."

Reframing is a quick-fix tool. When you add metaphors, language patterning, Meta-programs and the Spiral Coaching model techniques (see Chapter Seventeen), you will increase your potential for positive results.

If there is an underlying problem, reframing will expose it and give you the opportunity to use some of the other methods described in this book. However, reframing is a communications aid rather than a problem-solving technique, and it is not any form of intervention therapy.

Summary

- Some artists proclaim, "Change the frame and you alter the picture"
- Framing can be used to keep your client within the time allocated
- Reframing is a quick-fix tool
- Framing is setting the scene
- Reframing is changing the scene

Chapter Ten

Matters of State

*'State control can be restrictive for citizens of a dictatorship.
State control is equally liberating for clients of a coach'*

Synopsis

**When coaching, you must be aware of your own emotional state.
You select the most resourceful states for coaching and for your
clients. States can be anchored to auditory or visual triggers. You
can set anchors for your clients and you can trigger them at will
to produce the desired results or outcomes. If your present state
or the state of your client is not supporting the session, you can
quickly move into a desired resourceful state.**

A "state," for the purpose of this chapter, includes thoughts, physiology, emotions, mental pictures, sounds, tastes and breathing in
events separated by time. The connections of emotions and
thoughts are represented by our physical body and vice versa.

When a person is feeling physically low, very depressed and perhaps bursts into tears, they may be described as being in an "awful
state" or a "right state." Take a moment to consider your answers
to these questions:

- What puts you into a resourceful state?
- Can you perpetually be in a resourceful state?
- What state do you need to be in when talking to your clients
  and how can you ensure that you are there?
- What is a state?
- Are you in control of your state?
- Can you change your state to a more resourceful one whenever
  you desire?

Understanding the significance of state control will help you to encourage your clients to change from a poor present state to a positive desired state so that they are more receptive to effective coaching.

Thought and external stimuli control states. They are connected to the physiological expression of thoughts. When you change your thoughts, you change your physiology. When you change your physiology, you change your state. Therefore, bad habitual emotional states can be stamped out and eliminated completely, just by changing the thoughts and physiology associated with them.

There will be occasions when clients will contact you in an "awful state." You will want to change this into a resourceful state before getting on with the coaching. Before you can change the states of your clients, you must be able to control your own.

Here is an example of how easy it is to be in control of your state. Think of a time when you were very happy and enjoyed feeling especially good. Concentrate. Once you have identified the event, spend a minute or two fully experiencing it. Hear the sounds you heard. Visualise clearly the things you noticed. Relive the memory as vividly as you can. Feel all the feelings. Recall the smells, tastes, sounds or sights that you experienced during the event. Notice how good you feel as you remember this event. Just enjoy it for a moment.

Has your breathing changed? Has your posture changed? Do you feel different now? If you answered yes, you have just changed your state. You have been, and still are, in control of your state. If you answered no, then fully imagine that you have just been told that you have won five million pounds. How would you feel? Until you can change your state, or at least believe that you are in control of how you feel, you will seriously reduce the impact that you can have on the lives of your clients.

Now try another experiment. Think back to a time when someone really annoyed you. It was a very uncomfortable experience. Imagine yourself back there again. What can you see, feel or hear in that memory? Do not spend long in this negative event. Become aware of how you feel now. Has your state changed? Has your posture or breathing changed?

Throughout the day, you unconsciously and continually change states. You move from one to another. You allow events to control how you feel. For example, imagine a morning when you are feeling great. Then you open your mail or newspaper and read something really depressing. It upsets you. Suddenly the telephone rings. It is your best friend inviting you to go on an all-expenses-paid cruise, the one that you have often dreamed of. Your state changes from a little upset to exuberant. You have allowed your own state to be changed by external events.

Now imagine that you are very upset, lonely, depressed, tearful, perhaps recently parted from a loved one. It is a Saturday night and you are watching television, feeling very sorry for yourself. The lottery results are announced. You check your ticket. Your numbers have won a major prize. Do you think this would rapidly change your state? Of course it would. An outside stimulus would have changed your state.

You need to be in control of your own state in order consistently to deliver enthusiastic and energetic coaching sessions to your clients. Controlling your emotional state is essential to attaining true professionalism as a coach, because all effective skills flow from your state of mind.

A vitally important part of preparing for a coaching session is to establish a personal, resourceful state, and then to maintain it throughout the session. As a result, your coaching will flow with inspired communication.

Clients will fluctuate between states during your coaching sessions and your skill will be to elicit and maintain resourceful states from your clients throughout the entire session. To help you consistently achieve state control there is a technique called "anchoring," which is described later in this chapter.

So how do you select your states? First identify the state to which you wish to elicit, and then devise a plan to create it. Fascination is a resourceful state for a client. So assume for a moment that fascination is the state you would like to elicit from your client. There are many books written on how to elicit states but one great method that I use has not yet been written about.

I learned this method from an outstanding old coach. He guarded this technique secretly and jealously, for he believed it was the sole key to his entire success. One day he came to me and told me he had chosen me as the new scholar of his method. He painstakingly gave me the details. The old man was very particular that I should absolutely carefully follow the rules and regulations of this technique. The method is quite simple. I have often used it and it has given me success beyond my wildest dreams. The old man said it was my decision to choose whether to reveal it or to keep it secret. The last time I saw him, a very peculiar thing happened.

Are you captivated to discover what the technique is – or what happened to the old man? Would this information be useful to you? Are you curious to know whether the technique would help you to achieve success? Are you fascinated to know whether I have included the secret in this book?

Ask yourself whether my story made you feel fascinated, curious, captivated and inquisitive, or evoked any other interested type of state. If so, how did that happen? Read the paragraph again and you will notice how this change of state occurred. It is relatively easy to elicit resourceful states from your clients but it involves a certain amount of planning and practice. You can also change the state of your clients by telling them a story or a metaphor (see Chapter Sixteen).

A week before I wrote this I arrived at my favourite London hotel. It was very late and I was tired after a full day delivering a management programme, followed by a long journey. On arrival at reception, the clerk said there was no reservation for me. Two days before, I had overheard my assistant making this reservation and specifically stating I would be arriving late. I told the clerk, so he checked again. Still no reservation. To assist the clerk with his "customer-care skills," I asked if there were any spare rooms available. He checked again and could not find any.

"What can you do for me?" I asked. The clerk replied, "Nothing." I suggested, a little curtly, that he should call the duty manager. Eventually, an hour later, I was given a previously nonexistent, vacant room. Has anything like this ever happened to you? How did you feel? Can you remember the outcome?

I forgot to mention that the room the duty manager assigned to me was an executive suite. My breakfast order arrived along with a complimentary bottle of Krug champagne, a box of chocolates and a bouquet of flowers along with an apology note. How did I feel in the morning? Imagine for a moment this happened to you. How would you have felt?

In the above metaphor I was aiming to elicit in you a state of frustration followed by closely associated states of relief and happiness.

If you have a client who is nervous or excitable and you need to relax them, you need to change their state. To elicit the state of relaxation, start by asking your client to think of a time when they felt really relaxed. Ask them to remember a soothing bath, for example, and then question them about the warmth of the water, the smell of the soap, the silence or the music they may have been hearing. Continue until you detect a change in breathing or voice tone, or a slowing in the pace of their speech. These are all signs that your client has gone into the state of relaxation.

Alternatively, you could describe in great detail, using all the five senses or the "preferred" sense (see Chapter Eleven), a time when you were completely relaxed. As clients will relax differently, think of various situations to use – possibly a massage, sunbathing, reading a book or listening to soothing music.

You can change states by simply asking people to remember a time when they felt the state you are trying to elicit. Ask them to think about the time in detail and to feel how they felt then. Ask questions about their memory to help increase the intensity of the state. Once your clients are fully into the memory, you can anchor that state for future use.

Anchoring is a process by which any stimulus is connected to, and triggers, a response. Anchors can occur naturally or can be set up intentionally. A common anchor/response is: hear the fire alarm/automatically leave the building – an auditory anchor. The alarm is the anchor and leaving the building is the response triggered by the anchor. A song or a piece of music that reminds you of a certain event is an anchor. When you hear the music you recall the feelings related to the event.

In the UK, during the 1990s, the words "If you like a lot of chocolate on your biscuit join our club" would automatically be connected with the Club brand of biscuits. This example is an auditory anchor to the product. The world of advertising uses the anchoring technique extensively, spending billions of pounds on visual or auditory anchors. These are unconsciously triggered when we enter shops. They encourage us to buy the advertised products.

Anchors are very powerful, which is why they are used in advertising so much. For example, if you see a tick mark (✔), it might remind you of Nike sportswear or Sure deodorant. Alternatively, a picture with a piece of purple fabric with a slit in it may remind you of Silk Cut cigarettes. The letters "WC" on signs anchors us to public conveniences.

Let's have a look at some visual anchors that you may be conditioned into using. Traffic signals are a good example of visual anchors that road users recognise and respond to. A person shaking their head from side to side generally means that they are not in agreement with what is said. Nodding the head up and down is the "Yes, I am in agreement" anchor.

An anchor can be anything that will access a response or an emotional state. Anchors can be created in two ways:

- by repetition (in the example of advertising)
- through an emotion that has attached itself to a stimulus

An emotional anchor is hearing a love song and attaching it to the first dance you had with a person you love. To anchor states where there are no obvious emotions attached to a stimulus you can use repetition to create the response. You repeat and repeat the stimulus until the desired response is achieved. This method of anchoring, when used to teach children, is known as learning by rote.

As a life coach, you need to be fully aware of the differences between resourceful or positive states and negative or non-resourceful states.

A negative state, in extreme, is a phobia like arachnophobia, claustrophobia or agoraphobia. In *The Family Guide to Homeopathy*,

Dr Andrew Lochie describes a phobia as a "disabling fear attached to a specific object or situation which is, on the face of it, not at all threatening."

Arachnophobia is a state that produces fear in people at the sight of spiders.

Trigger: See a spider

Response: Feel fear

This is a negative-state anchor!

Claustrophobia is the fear of confined spaces and agoraphobia the fear of open spaces. The sight of or the thought of spatial relationships to comfort and safety triggers both phobias.

A milder example of a negative-state anchor could be a hospital. Some people feel nervous or anxious when they have to go to the hospital or even visit a patient. They associate hospitals with fear or illness and, therefore, actually visiting or the thought of a hospital triggers the fear. Interestingly, this fear is usually associated before the person has ever been a patient in a hospital. Someone else describing his or her feelings or experiences has created the fear and this in turn has created the anchor that hospital equals pain.

You can select any states you require and anchor the state for recall in the future. You can choose a resourceful state, anchor it and trigger the anchor any time you need it. This is a very useful tool for coaching. You can also trigger states in your clients and anchor them. When you need a resourceful state for your clients you simply set off the trigger anchor and the response is the resourceful state.

Anchoring states is a three-step process:

> **Step One**: You decide the emotional state that you wish your clients to recall.
> **Step Two**: You put your client into the state.
> **Step Three**: You associate that state with an anchor or a stimulus.

This will allow you to bring back the state whenever you use that stimulus or anchor.

For instance, if you have chosen to create the state of enthusiasm in your client, when you know your client is fully associated into the state of enthusiasm, you can click a pen a couple of times. The next time you want to elicit the state of enthusiasm in your client, simply click the pen. If this does not elicit a strong state of enthusiasm, help the state to develop by reminding your client of the time they were enthusiastic. The two methods used simultaneously should work for you. To become proficient in anchoring, you will find it useful to enrol on an accredited Neuro-Linguistic Programming course.

Resourceful states are the key to outstanding performance. Some resourceful states you might want to elicit are enthusiasm, confidence, decision making, high energy, fascination, curiosity, interest, courage, determination, certainty.

To have instant access to these states, simply associate into the state and then anchor it. To access these states in your clients, anchor them. You will enable your clients to achieve goals far beyond their beliefs by utilising their resourceful states.

Summary

- You need to be in a resourceful state before, during and after a coaching session
- You can elicit resourceful states from your clients
- Anchoring is a technique for eliciting states
- Anchors can be consciously triggered or unconsciously triggered
- Clients will already be anchored to different states

Chapter Eleven

Representational Systems

'See and hear correctly to be in touch at the right time'

Synopsis

Representational systems describe modes of operation that humans use to perceive and record the events they experience. Representational systems are what we might call the 'navigational chart of events' not the event itself. Similarly, the navigational ocean charts are not the seas. All of us can, and do, use all of our senses to record events and recall them from memory. Although we move freely through the representational systems, we prefer to work in just one. These systems are based on our five senses. This chapter has focused on the main three systems: auditory, kinaesthetic and visual. Advanced coaches will identify the representational system of each client and respond in the same terms. This eases the communication process and reduces common barriers to relationship building.

Each human being processes information differently from another, by creating their own internal representation of an outside event. These internal representations are not the events themselves, but are the way the individual has interpreted them based on personal experiences of life and social conditioning.

For example, we all know that a navigational chart is not the sea. It is simply the representation of some of the key features of the oceans at the time the chart was drawn. NLP practitioners have a favourite saying for this: "The map is not the territory." The analogy of charting can be applied to the way that humans record events.

When an external event happens to us, we run our own perception of that event through internal processing. We create our own

'Navigational Chart of the Sea of Events,' which depends on the way we prefer to remember things. We store and remember events by making an internal representation through our senses. The predominant senses we use during these storage and retrieval processes are visual, auditory and kinaesthetic. To a smaller extent, the olfactory (smell) and taste senses are also used, but their impact is not significant enough to be examined in this chapter.

Although you use all of your senses all of the time, there are occasions when you use one sense predominately. When listening to a music concert on the radio you would principally be using your auditory sense. If you were having a shower, you would be predominantly accessing your kinaesthetic sense, as you would be feeling the sensation of the warm water caressing your body. If you visited an art gallery, your primary visual sense would be used.

Although we are capable of using all three of these senses, there is always a tendency to favour just one of them when we are recording and recalling events. During the information storage process, some people store events as pictures and images, some by the sounds heard (the person speaking at the time – teacher, boss or coach) and others by how they felt at the time. Awareness of the information-processing system that your clients prefer to use will help you to build instant rapport.

Your auditory clients will remember a conversation word for word, without leaving out a single syllable. Your kinaesthetic clients will store information by how they felt at the time – whether they felt that the information was true, how they felt about the information when it was being given to them and how they felt about the speaker. Your visual clients will construct a snapshot of events like a photographer or an artist, storing the total image away for recall.

Every single coaching client will favour a specific sense. Understanding this principle enables you to hook (a kinaesthetic word) on to the interests of the three main types of representational systems your clients will be using. Then you can use this knowledge to great advantage, as it will increase your client's understanding of each coaching session.

Your clients can be divided into three main categories, which correspond to these major representational systems.

Auditory clients will hear the sound of your voice in their head when they are being coached and they will be able to recall the conversation in its entirety, including tonality and any other background sounds. These clients can be slower with their recall but they will retrieve the conversations exactly as if they were playing back a recording.

Kinaesthetic clients will experience sensations and have feelings about the coaching session they are taking part in. They recall their feelings first, followed by the information recorded. This is the slowest form of processing.

Visual clients will record and construct pictures or images of their coaching sessions and all other life experiences. They have instant recall because they bring back the whole picture instantly.

When coaching you need to be aware of which system each client is using. You do this by listening carefully to their language patterns in conversation.

Your clients will use their preferred representational system to describe events to you. This is a great opportunity for you to identify their preferred representational systems. Then, by using the same system when it is your turn to speak, you will enhance your connection with your clients. The principle works on the basis that people like people like themselves, and it is a valuable tool in establishing rapport.

Auditory clients use sentences such as:

* I *hear* what you're saying
* That *sounds* like a good idea to me
* I want you to *listen* to my idea on the subject

Kinaesthetic clients are more likely to say:

* *Hold* that thought
* I don't *grasp* that

- Oh that doesn't *feel* right to me

Visual clients will more often say:

- I can't *see* what it is you are trying to get across
- I get the *picture*
- Is there a different *perspective* on this idea?

Remember that your clients can, and will, use all of these systems, but you will note that, as the conversation proceeds, each has a primary representational system that they rely on above the others.

In 1979 John Grinder and Richard Bandler – whom we met in Chapter Eight – developed the theory that professionals in human resource development could increase the trust and rapport with their client or trainee by using that individual's primary language system. They concluded this by listening to the words the trainee used and then used exactly the same words in the sentences they used for the training. They believed it was possible that trainees learned best when the content was presented to them using their primary representational systems. When coaching, use this knowledge of representational systems: listen for the preferred system, then use the same one to increase your communicating effectiveness.

Your auditory clients will remember the sounds, so it is important to change your tone, pitch and pace when coaching them. Use descriptions that relate to all forms of sound, including musical terminology. Ask them if the ideas sound good to them. Ask them to tell you about their goals.

Your kinaesthetic clients respond best when they actually experience things: for example, when they have completed a goal that you both agreed on. When you follow up on the tasks previously given, ask them how they felt about it? Use words that describe feelings throughout your conversation to involve and inspire these clients. Ask them how concrete their goals feel.

Your visual clients need visual terms. When giving a visual client a task to complete it would help to describe the results in pictorial form. Ask them to describe in detail what it would look like for them. Ask them what they see as their ultimate outcomes. Tell them you will show them how they can fulfil their dreams.

When coaching, if your preferred representational system is visual and your client has a preferred system of kinaesthetic, there will be some difficulties in the information transfer from you to your client.

There are some other clues that can help you detect the system that each client prefers.

Auditory Clients

Auditory clients tend to be relaxed when they sit in a chair. They tilt their heads to one side slightly when listening. They may be breathing from the middle of their body using a regulated smooth pace. They are generally of medium build and can be well dressed. They are just as likely to be casually dressed, as clothing holds no great importance to them.

Auditory clients are renowned for talking to themselves and are easily distracted by noise or sounds from outside the room. If they hear drilling outside or a telephone ringing in the background, they lose concentration. They will hear all the background sounds no matter how low these may be. It is important that the coach make sure there are no auditory distractions for these clients. If you play background music, be sure that it is popular with your client.

They memorise predominantly through their auditory sense and this means they absorb information sequentially. Your visual clients will memorise many things at one time but your auditory clients need information presented in a sequential manner because they can hear only one sound at a time. This also means that they are slower in processing and recalling from memory. It does not mean that they are less intelligent than your visual clients: it simply means that they process information differently.

When coaching your auditory clients you need to take great care with the words you use. Select them with absolute attention to detail. Use simple language and words that have only one meaning. Always summarise what has been agreed and get your client to repeat back to you what they believe they heard. Your auditory clients will remember every single word you speak and be able to repeat conversations you had with them over a year ago – verbatim.

It is not enough to select your words with care: you also need to focus on the tonality that you use when delivering them. These clients will take meanings from your tone more quickly than you can say what you wish to say. If you are remotely tired, bored or uninterested, or your attention has lapsed while you are speaking to them, they will know instantly.

You will be a lucky coach if they let you know that they noticed your lapse, for they are more likely to tell other people and destroy your referral system. They are superstars when it comes to listening for meaning. Unless you are auditory as well, you stand no chance against them. So beware, and take special care about how you say things and exactly what you say, because your auditory clients will be listening with supersensitive antennae.

Here are some phrases an auditory client could use:

- that sounds good
- let's talk to her
- I'd like to listen to that
- did you hear that?
- it's been great talking to you
- blabbermouth
- give an account of yourself
- tuned in
- loud and clear
- manner of speaking
- within hearing
- word for word
- hidden message
- rings a bell

Kinaesthetic Clients

Kinaesthetic clients will tend to be heavily built or heavier boned. They may breathe from the bottom of the lungs so that you will see their stomach going in and out. They are usually very relaxed and could lean back or drape themselves over a desk or chair. They typically talk in a very slow manner, pronouncing words individually one after the other. The reason is that they are trying to get a feel for how things are, according to themselves. Feelings take much longer to process than sounds or pictures.

One of the biggest mistakes you can make is to underestimate the intelligence of a kinaesthetic client because of their slowness of speech or the slow pace at which they process information. They are constantly passing the information over their feelings and this takes time. It does not mean they are dull-minded or do not understand. Always give your kinaesthetic clients plenty of time to digest what you have discussed. Be very slow to ask them if they have understood. If you are a visual coach and you have a kinaesthetic client you will need to exercise huge amounts of control to create a bonding relationship. It will be your greatest challenge.

Your kinaesthetic clients will respond well to physical rewards: for example, if you pat them on the back. If you are coaching over the telephone you need to say only, "Pat yourself on the back" and your kinaesthetic client will immediately respond. They are very "touchy-feely," so they are likely to touch you if you coach them face-to-face. Generally speaking they are physical in their nature. They want to experience things and they really enjoy physical contact. If you do not like to be touched by strangers, avoid kinaesthetic clients, or deal with them only over the telephone. They will be quick to notice if you wince or withdraw your arm when they touch you. They will experience this as a personal rebuff, repulsion or rejection and will not respond to your coaching positively.

Here are some phrases that a kinaesthetic client could use

- I can't get a handle on that
- we'd better get in touch with …
- hold on to that idea

- let me walk you through this
- all washed up
- come to grips with
- hand in hand
- cool, calm and collected
- hot-headed
- hold it!
- sharp as a razor
- pull some strings
- start from scratch
- slipped through my hands

Visual Clients

Clients with a visual primary representational system will stand or sit with their heads and bodies erect, their face and eyes usually held upwards, and they may be taking short breaths from the top of their lungs.

They may sit on the edge of their chair or sit forward in their chair. Quite often they are neat, well groomed and orderly and would have organised the space in front of them neatly. They would be sitting in a "neat" or precise manner. Their actions are deliberate. Visual clients memorise by seeing images in their minds and are not distracted by noise. Quite often, if someone is good at spelling, this may be indicative of their being predominately visual. If you send them any written material, either by post or e-mail, you should always check the spelling especially carefully if you want to keep their respect.

They will have difficulty in remembering long oral instructions and explanations, as their minds will tend to wander. When a visual client is given instructions on getting to a specific location, they will find it difficult to remember. To ensure their safe arrival, give some kind of visual picture for them to follow. Talk in highly descriptive terms of the colour and shapes of houses, monuments, pubs and visually recognisable features.

When you discuss your visual client's goals, ask them to describe the goal clearly, what they see, what the result will look like and their picture of it. They may be inclined to speak very quickly and jump from subject to subject with ease. They may breathe quickly, like panting without the noise. They want fast responses and the coach needs to keep up with their conversational pace. If the coach is slower in pace, breathing and recall, the visual client could lose connectivity.

How they look is important for visual people; they will be smartly dressed. The way you look and dress will affect whether they choose you as their coach.

Here are some phrases a visual client could use.

- see you later
- let's focus on this
- I want to look at it
- it's a bit hazy
- picture this
- watch out
- it appears to me
- did you notice that
- an eyeful
- mental image
- photographic memory
- showing off
- pretty as a picture
- short-sighted

When you first speak to a prospective client, use a language that incorporates all three representational systems. This will give you time to recognise their primary representational system without risking alienation. Once you know their primary representational system you should switch your language to match theirs.

You probably incorporate all three representational systems into your own language. Have a *look* at the way in which you present your information, and you will get a *feeling* for whether it is right. If you *listen* to yourself, you will notice whether you use all three systems in your coaching style already. Ask a friend to listen for the key words in your vocabulary. Remember, though: your friend will notice more key words from their own primary representational system and this may bias the feedback.

Here are some words and phrases used by each representational system.

Auditory	Kinaesthetic	Visual
question	scrape	picture
listen	get hold of	look
tune in	catch on	see
make music	touch	appear
be all ears	tap into	vision
rings a bell	unfeeling	dawn
deaf	solid	crystal clear
mellifluous	throw out	hazy
hear	grasp	view
be heard	turn around	foggy
dissonance	concrete	reveal
silence	get a handle	imagine
sounds	slip through	illuminate
harmonise	hard	show
clangour	feel	focused

Learning these words will help you to identify the representational systems quickly and make it easier for you to build instant rapport with your clients.

Here is an example of the confusion that can arise from mismatched systems. Take a visual client and a kinaesthetic coach:

CLIENT: I can't see how this coaching's going to be of any benefit to me.
COACH: Why do you feel like that?
CLIENT: I don't have a clear picture of where we're going or what use this is going to be for me.
COACH: Don't worry. I feel that you'll soon get to grips with it.
CLIENT: I'd like you to show me how this will be of benefit to me so that I can get it crystal clear in my mind.

The coach and the client are using two different representational systems. In this case the client will think that the coach cannot *show* things *clearly*. The coach would probably *feel* that the client is frustrating all attempts to *reach* the goals and the result will be bewildering for both parties. This could lead to a breakdown in communication and a loss of client and business.

Now consider a similar conversation, in which the coach matches the client's visual preference:

CLIENT : I can't see how this coaching's going to be of any benefit to me.

COACH : I *notice* that you *looked* confused when I was giving out that work assignment, and it *appeared* to me that you didn't get the full *picture*.

CLIENT : If you could give me an *overview* then I might be able to *focus* on how this work assignment fits into it.

COACH : Yes, I see what you mean. So what we can do is to *look* at this from different angles and get a new *perspective* on how this will fit into the overall grand *picture* for you. Would that help?

The client and the coach are both using visual language and therefore building rapport. The client will get more from this coaching style because both parties are seeing things from the same perspective. When you identify the primary representational system of a client and can use the same language, you will accelerate the effectiveness of the coaching process and increase the number of successful outcomes.

When you begin your coaching session with a new client, it may not be easy for you to identify their representational system. Incorporate all three systems to resolve this initial problem: "I'm going to *show* you how we can get the results you are *looking* for. Does this *sound* interesting to you; do you *feel* comfortable working this way?"

Spend a few moments thinking of different ways you can adopt to introduce your own coaching sessions using each of the three main representational systems. You should write them down and practise saying them until you become fluent and fluid. Clients will recognise instantly if you are reading from a script and they will not be impressed.

Summary

- We all speak using representational systems
- Each of us uses a primary or preferred representational system
- The main representational systems are auditory, kinaesthetic and visual
- Coaches need to converse in each representational system
- Mismatched representational systems will lead to misunderstanding and difficulties in rapport building

Chapter Twelve

Fundamental Rapport Skills

'Rapport is the natural state for humans striving to build a relationship'

Synopsis

To build strong client relationships you must be in rapport. Match and mirror clients' construction of language, body language and amplification language. When building the bridges of rapport you must always think in terms of your clients' needs, not your own needs or preferences. A smile reduces the distance between two people and a handshake can enhance the process or squeeze it to death.

Rapport is the bridge that we build between our clients and ourselves and over which all communication must pass. It is therefore imperative to build each bridge with the materials that the client is prepared to walk across. To continue with the metaphor (see Chapter Sixteen) for a moment, there is little use constructing a bridge of cypress wood if the person on the other side is a pyromaniac. They will burn the bridge as soon as you construct it. A brick bridge without cement to hold it together may initially impress but, as soon as anyone attempts to cross, it will collapse.

The moral of this metaphor is that, when building the bridges of rapport, you must always think in terms of your client's needs and not your own preferences.

"Rapport, in fact, is the foundation of all excellent communication," Robert Smith wrote in his book, *Up Your Aspirations*. As life coaches we must forever strive to establish excellent communication with our clients.

The different ways of building rapport can be grouped under the three headings:

- construction of language
- body language
- amplification language

In Chapter Eleven, we looked at some of the aspects of construction of language in the representational systems that people use. When you are coaching a visual client you must construct a bridge using visual words. Auditory clients will remember the sounds, therefore it is important to construct a bridge of tone, pitch and pace. Kinaesthetic clients need to feel that the bridge is solid and safe. Essential communication skills as they apply to the construction of language are covered in greater detail in Chapter Five.

As body language plays a major part in the way we communicate, it needs special attention when we are building rapport. It is said that the shortest distance between two people is a smile – so always smile when you meet your clients. A smile conveys various messages but you are in no position to control the interpretation of any of them.

However, it is generally accepted that a smile means that you are happy to meet them, you are relaxed, confident, friendly, open and honest – or any combination of these. Your smile must be genuine because your client will instantly be aware of a forced one and may interpret it to mean that you are untrustworthy, questionable, capricious or dubious. None of these is helpful in establishing the relationships that you need to build a coaching practice.

As you smile, offer your hand for the traditional handshake. If you are the first to offer your hand it lets the other person know what is expected and sets the scene. It shows that you are confident and prepared to take the lead. It may also convey that you are warm and welcoming. There are many interpretations in the offer of a handshake.

Take care when shaking hands. If you have been to university or business school you have probably been taught to shake hands firmly but not tightly, and this is safe advice. A better handshake is one that matches what you are given. So, if you get a strong grasping handshake, just return the favour with matching strength and force. If you receive a limp handshake, just return with a soft handshake that nearly matches the limpness but conveys a slightly stronger personality.

The reason you do not match like for like in the limp situation is because they are coming to you for coaching. They are more likely to create rapport with you if they feel you are able to lead them out of their weakness. A firm grasp with this client would have the reverse effect – it could instantly make them fearful of you and building rapport from that moment will be a struggle.

The initial few minutes of the first meeting are the most crucial, so make sure you are concentrating on the other person. Do not show off and avoid trying to dominate. Give a genuine smile, extend the hand for a handshake and deliver it according to the client's response. Compliment or admire something about your client – you must genuinely appreciate what you are admiring. A jazzy tie, a brooch, a colour of nail polish, anything you like. We all like to receive a genuine compliment.

Imagine for a moment you are observing three couples in a restaurant sitting at different tables. None of them is speaking. One couple have recently met and they are in love; another couple have been together for several years and the relationship has broken down; the last couple have been together over fifteen years and are comfortable in each other's company. Could you identify which is which? Of course you could, because we are natural experts at reading body language.

The couple in love will be matching and mirroring each other in every way. When one drinks the other drinks; they will be leaning towards each other and their actions could be described as a dance. They would be in harmony in all aspects.

The couple with a broken relationship will be sitting in opposing positions, possibly with their bodies turned partly away from each other. There would be little eye contact and each would move independently from the other. There would be no synchronicity, no dance. You could cut the atmosphere with a knife.

The final couple would be sitting in a relaxed manner with open body language and, although not as intense as couple number one, they would be synchronising their movements and would have good eye contact. Each would be mirroring or matching the other's body position.

Mirroring is when the other person moves or looks like your reflection. If you lift your right arm they would lift their left arm. *Matching* body language is what happens when you lift your right arm, and they also lift their right arm. Usually the movements take place one shortly after the other rather than simultaneously, unless the couple are deeply in rapport.

When you meet your clients you need to get into rapport with them quickly, demonstrating mirroring or matching subtly. Rapport is the natural state for humans striving to build a relationship. The only time you need to be aware and to adjust your body language is during conversations that are not achieving agreements.

As soon as you become aware of communication difficulties, pay conscious attention to your body language, adjust, mirror or match your client to rebuild body rapport. Facial expressions offer further opportunities to build rapport by mirroring.

We looked briefly at changing breathing rates for effect in Chapter Five, but one way of helping to achieve rapport through matching is to observe your client's breathing rate and make yours correspond. And then there is our blinking rate – yet another matching technique for rapport building. We all blink our eyes at different rates and sometimes the more subtle approach of matching your client's blink rate is easier than changing your body position or matching breathing rate.

Amplification language concerns the volume, pitch, tone and speed at which the client speaks. We all have a preferred style of amplification, just as we have a preferred representational system. Generally these two systems are closely linked. Remember that clients who process information with a visual filter usually breathe quickly from the top of their chests and speak quickly with a high pitch. Auditory clients will have a wide range of tone and pitch. They will modulate their voice like a song and the pace will be smooth and regular. Kinaesthetic clients will be slow and low in volume, pitch and tone.

You can also match your client's Meta-programs, which are described in Chapter Fifteen.

The bridge of common experiences is often used to build rapport. Conversational small talk starts this process off. "Did you have a good journey?" You respond according to what they say. For example, if they say their journey was easy, you would respond with, "Yes, there doesn't seem to be so much traffic today." If they say they had a bad journey because a tyre burst, you would match that with something like, "I'm sorry to hear that. It's a real inconvenience when something like that happens," which indicates that you have had a similar experience.

Rapport building is one of the most natural activities of human relationships and we are all gifted with the ability. It is when you are not getting the responses you need for a strong client–coach relationship that a review of your bridge-building materials can make all the difference to establishing rapport.

Summary

- Match and mirror body language
- Breathing and blinking rates need attention
- Amplification language matching builds rapport
- Representational systems should be matched
- Common experiences can be shared

Chapter Thirteen

The Milton Model

*'The deliberate use of artfully vague language can
benefit the client and the coach'*

Synopsis

**The Milton H. Erickson model of artfully vague language can
assist communication between the life coach and the client.
Nominalisations, ambiguity, unspecified referential index, dele-
tion, word linking, causal statements, mind reading, universal
quantifiers, modal operators, presuppositions and embedded
commands are adapted for effective use by the coach.**

Milton H. Erickson (1902–80) was widely revered as the initial
president of the American Society for Clinical Hypnosis. He
moved the whole process of hypnosis forward by achieving amazing results in hitherto unheard-of brief periods of time. Some com-
mentators suggest that his practice was the touchstone that led
Bandler and Grinder to formulate NLP. They used the Milton
Model to describe their use of his language patterns and related
techniques.

There is a vast library of Erickson's works. In this chapter we focus
on his ideas of "artfully vague language." Paradoxically, this is a
style that can actually help client-and-coach communications. He
initially developed this model to assist with his hypnotherapy
clients. Erickson deliberately constructed sentences that had no
actual meaning. The listener, however, would give the words
meaning according to their own reality, based on their personal life
experiences, beliefs and values. Here we develop the pattern as it
applies to the coaching context.

When a coach is artfully vague, the client will respond with their
own answers. These answers will be best suited to the client's own
needs to help them reach their goals. It reduces the possibilities for

the coach inadvertently to put obstacles or extraneous and inappropriate suggestions in the way of client success.

Artfully vague language construction lets your clients take what they need from your words in a way that is most appropriate for them. It involves directing your client's attention to something without actually spelling it out.

These words should direct your client to go "inside," and search for their own meaning from their own reality. It is like giving your client an empty glass and letting them fill it with whatever they need to achieve whatever they want.

Nominalisations

Using the Milton Model during coaching is about ensuring that your clients take their individual meaning from the coaching sessions rather than have you deliver that meaning. You achieve this by leaving out information or using words that have many interpretations and are known in NLP as nominalisations.

This will be clearer if you consider this example: "Research shows that people can watch videos and change."

What does this mean? Who were the researchers? What was the research? Who was researched? What videos were used? How did the people change? What did they change into?

The beauty of using artfully vague sentences is that your client will make up the missing details and therefore create specific meanings. During the next minute, consider the following sentence and create a picture in your mind.

"Fat old Pat is wearing a new hat."

Now answer these questions:

- How fat was the Pat in your picture?
- How old was Pat?
- Was Pat male or female?

- What type of hat was Pat wearing?
- What colour was the hat?
- What colour was Pat's skin?
- What clothes did Pat have on?
- Could you see Pat's hair? If yes, what colour was it?
- What was the colour of Pat's eyes?
- What location did you put Pat in?
- Was Pat standing or sitting?

These questions show that there are many different ways to interpret "artfully vague" language. Now that you have the idea, let us consider how you can apply it during a coaching session.

Using "you can" in a sentence allows your clients the opportunity to do something without your giving them a command. They believe that they are given choices and therefore they rarely object to any of your suggestions.

Erickson used such language to distract and occupy a patient's conscious mind so that he could then access the resources of the unconscious mind. Using ambiguity is a good way of doing this and is very useful in coaching.

Fortune-tellers and palm readers have successfully used ambiguity as a means of getting the public to interpret their ambiguous forecasts as being personal to each receiver. Read this extract from Jonathan Cainer's horoscope prediction in the *Daily Express*:

Libra (Sep 24–Oct 23)

Sometimes we just don't realise how much we are holding together until we take our energy and attention away from a certain situation. Then we find out whether it really has a life of its own – or whether it only exists because we are giving so much of ourselves to it. You have turned your back, just for a moment, on a set of arrangements. They now seem to be falling apart. This tells you something valuable. You can't live comfortably under a roof that only stays in position when you personally, physically hold up the walls.

What does this mean? Who knows? A cynic would see it as a load of mumbo-jumbo, but the regular reader will have become expert at seeing this vague forecast as a personal message. It is a message that only they can interpret. And that is the beautiful effectiveness of artfully vague language.

A palm reader or tarot practitioner, using vague language, might say, "I can see from your hand [or the cards] that you've been through some tough times."

This is brilliantly ambiguous. Most people will have experienced some hardship in their lives. What does "tough" mean? How tough is tough? How many times is "times"? Each individual customer will internalise this comment and will be able to find periods in their life that enable them to make it personally meaningful. In many instances, people consult a fortune-teller during a period when things are going badly for them. Armed with this knowledge the fortune-teller can use that sentence or something like it with impunity.

There is a secondary power. The customer really wants the sentence to apply to them. They have paid for the consultation and this generally means that they have committed themselves to the value of the service being given. It is therefore important for them to find benefits to justify the price. They have a driving desire for proof that their decision to spend has been justified and that they are not being conned.

Your clients will have the same underlying commitment to finding value from your coaching sessions. This secondary influence gives power to any artfully vague language you use.

Suppose, during a coaching session, you said, "I know you've been through some tough times and, because of these times, you are stronger and have many useful resources which you can now use to help you find the best way of achieving your outcomes."

Your client may feel that you truly understand their situation and will be aware that you know that they have had problems – in reality you may have absolutely no idea about their situation and no knowledge about their problems. How does this work?

It works because your client will want you to understand, to confirm the wisdom of their commitment. They will perform an internal search looking for examples of tough times in their lives. They will match what you have said with any experiences that they find. In doing so, they will think you have some hidden talent that gives you insight into their personal background.

Ambiguity is a close relative of artfully vague language. Say to your client, "I was wondering [this starts your client wondering] about times when you easily accomplished a task." Your client now wanders about – and wonders off into – their model of the world and finds examples of events to match this sentence. You use these events to make their future tasks and goals seem easier when they compare the essential skills required for the achievement of both the vague or ambiguously suggested "past task" with their new "future task," needing similar skills for completion.

Unspecified Referential Index

Milton Erickson also used the "unspecified referential index" as a means of triggering individual interpretation. For example, "People like being coached" or "This is easy." Such phrases are similar to nominalisations but the information about the noun is missing. They can be used when discussing people, things or feelings when you want your client to personalise the sentence and give you leverage.

Deliberate vagueness can give your clients the freedom to fill in the blank space. For example, "I know that you are growing" is a great response immediately after your client tells you about the completion of a successful task. The significance of this sentence is that your client will know which element of their life is growing. They will also believe that you know which element is growing and how it is growing. You do not need to know.

This is an important point when you use these techniques. Not only do you not need to know, but it is very important that your client should do the interpretation and that you be not involved at any point. The power is in the fact that the client knows and can identify with the sentence.

Word Linking or Causal Statements

An additional technique of "word linking" or "causal statements" uses the power of implication by creating a relationship or link between two separate situations or actions. This may seem a little complicated but it is easy. (The last sentence was an example of an unspecified referential index.) There are some useful linking words for coaching and the most advantageous words are "means," "causes" and "makes."

- "Being healthy means you can achieve at work"
- "Working long hours causes serious illness"
- "Coaching makes people successful"

If you have a client who is a little reluctant to take some action, it is helpful to construct a sentence with a linking word. If your client is reluctant to work on health, for example, you could use a statement that links health to wealth or poor health to serious illness. Your choice of which link to use may be dependant on which Meta-program – an "away-from" or a "towards" Meta-program – your client utilises in the context of their health (see Chapter Fifteen).

The use of causal statements or word linking can be "time-based," "conjunction" or "causal." Time-based words establish a connection between two points. In coaching, the most useful are "as," "when," "during" and "while." You can use these to connect things that are concurrently happening although they have no natural linkage. For example: "As you tell me about your goals they become clearer and easier to achieve."

This sentence connects goals, clarity and ease with the situation of your client talking to you. To increase the effectiveness of your language you can stack the causal statements by starting with simple conjunction – using "and" as the linking word – then move seamlessly into time-based and complete the sentence with a causality statement.

"While you are listening to my words *and* beginning to feel easier about coaching, *and* as you notice how beneficial coaching is, you

can become a client. Which *means* that you can benefit from the successes that are sure to follow."

This sentence in the cold light of reading may seem clumsy but, as you practise using it, you will find that it works well. Clients will be able to list the benefits of life coaching without any help or prompting from you.

Mind Reading

Perhaps you think that this all seems too contrived and possibly a little puzzling. So now is the best time to introduce "mind reading." This form of language construction can increase your credibility as a coach. "Mind reading" is achieved by the use of generalisations, speaking as if you already knew what the client is thinking or feeling: "You may be wondering what's involved in life coaching."

If you say this during the first contact call, it is probably going to be true, because they made the call to find out more about life coaching. The fact that you have implied that you know they are wondering is taken as meaning that you understand them, and so this helps you to build rapport and enhance your credibility as an understanding coach.

Universal Quantifier

Coaching can also use "universal quantifiers," which are generalisations you present as facts. For example: "*Everyone* knows coaching works" or "*All* the skills you need are easily learned."

A great universal quantifier for you to use would be, "*Everyone* has *all* the skills they need to succeed."

This sentence has two universal quantifiers and one nominalisation – "succeed." Sometimes your clients, typically those with a "specific" Meta-program (see Chapter Fifteen), will challenge you when you use universal quantifiers. This is fine: just agree with them and move swiftly on to another topic.

Modal Operators

Modal operators of possibility and necessity give you the opportunity to discover whether your client believes that they have a choice or absence of choice in the situation. When there is an absence of choice they are inclined to use phrases such as "I must." "I ought to," "I should," "It's my duty," "I can't do that" – or others that restrict them from taking any action. The most effective way to deal with these modes of operation is to ask the question, "What would happen if you did?"

Usually your clients are surprised to discover that they do have the answers within. Then one of the best things that can happen is that you help your client to discover that they are running an old pattern of behaviour, which no longer serves them. Then you show them ways of changing this pattern. This discovery is a great release for the client and one of the joys of coaching.

The modal operator of possibility used by clients allows them always to find an alternative way of looking at things or offer several different ways to approach a problem. Your challenge is to determine whether they are genuinely comparing options or just avoiding taking action.

Presuppositions

Using presuppositions is one of the most powerful language patterns for coaching. Presuppositions are used when you do not want your client to question you. You simply presuppose that your point exists in the statement. It makes it harder for your client to challenge your comments.

"Peter saw the boat." What is presupposed in these four words? They presuppose that two things exist: something called Peter and something called boat. Presuppositions also work when stated in the negative. "Peter did not see the boat." The implied existence of Peter and boat is the same.

Here are some more examples to drive the point home.

"When you have been promoted you can use the extra money to ..." This sentence presupposes that the client will be promoted and that the promotion will bring with it extra money.

"When you experience the benefits of your success, you ..." The presuppositions in this sentence are that there are benefits and that there will be success.

"We've talked about the benefits of life coaching. So which service do you know will be better for you, the gold or the platinum service?" The presupposition of the benefits is in this sentence along with the presupposition that the client is going to buy and needs only to decide which service to buy. It rules out the decision of whether to buy or not.

"It's been a long time since anyone's really listened to you, hasn't it?" The presuppositions are that there is a period of time, that no one else listens and that the speaker is listening.

"In the past, when you couldn't lose weight ..." This presupposes that not losing weight is now a thing of the past and that in the present and future your client can lose weight.

Embedded Commands

Embedded commands or questions are *very easy for you to understand* and are also a great tool for life coaching. You simply give a command indirectly within the sentence or the question, as in the italicised words above.

"I'm curious about how *you think I can help you*." "What is really interesting to me is when did *you decide to hire a coach*?"

First, be very clear about the outcome that you are looking for and then construct the sentence with that outcome stated within it. When coaching a client who has demonstrated previous difficulty in understanding an idea or instruction, always give them the embedded command – "You will find this clear and easy to understand" – then tell them what it is that you want them to find easy to understand. This procedure sets the scene and puts your client into the right positive state of mind about the task.

Beware, though: the antithesis is also true. When you use sentences that include "difficult," "worry" and words with similar connotations, you are embedding difficulties. Avoid sentences such as, "I know you won't find this difficult" and "Please don't worry about ...." Your client will automatically find it difficult or they will start to worry, simply because you have given them the instruction to do so. Always select the words you use to enhance the achievement of your client's outcome. If you want your client to remember something, use "remember" instead of telling them, "Don't forget to ...." Take care about what you say to your clients and they will take care of you.

This chapter offers a brief exploration of the Milton Model of artfully vague language and some of its related techniques. It is only a start for your discovery of its great advantages for a coach.

All outstanding coaches use these effective techniques. You may now be asking yourself, "How important will this model be when I use it in my coaching practice?" You are assured of finding the answers you need.

Summary

- When a coach is artfully vague the client will respond with his or her own answers
- Nominalisations are process words
- "People like being coached" or "this is easy" are examples of unspecified referential index
- Presuppositions increase effectiveness of coaching
- "I'm curious about how *you think I can help you.*"

Chapter Fourteen

Meta-language Patterns

*'A coach knows the strengths and weaknesses of
language and uses each to great effect'*

Synopsis

The Meta-language programmes, like the Milton Model of art-fully vague language, can assist the life coach and client to communicate. It identifies when a client is using nominalisations, unspecified nouns and verbs, cause-and-effect statements, mind reading, universal quantifiers, modal operators and presuppositions – by challenging the client to specify exactly what they mean. Meta-language also is a great tool for coaching, especially if you use presuppositions and embedded commands.

Like the Milton Model described in Chapter Thirteen, a Meta-language pattern describes a particular way of using language to create a desired outcome. But that is where the similarity ends.

The Milton Model is deliberately "artfully vague," to lead your clients into making their own interpretations of what you say. Then they believe that the ideas are theirs and usually commit to ensuring that they achieve their goals.

Meta-language patterns, however, are precise and they utilise both the strengths and weaknesses of language. They also offer a safeguard to prevent you from assuming that you know exactly what the other person means when they use a word.

In Chapter Five you were offered an extract from *The Hobbit* to demonstrate how the greeting "Good morning" could be interpreted in several different ways. When you use Meta-language patterns, there is no such scope for interpretation.

The intended outcome of this chapter is to stimulate your interest in this technique for the coaching process and to show how you can use language to help you achieve results with your clients.

Think for a minute about the way you communicate. There are bound to be occasions when you think one thing and say something different. Consider a situation where you want to tell someone that they are "an idiot" but, because they happen to be your boss, you say instead, "I think you may have misunderstood what I was saying" – even though you are well aware that this is an example of distorting and generalising.

If someone asked you directions to the supermarket and you explained how to get there exactly as you thought about it, the directions would be long and complicated and would probably not make sense to the other person. In your mind you would probably notice Fred's house, the new neighbours' red car, a broken paving slab and so on. But you would not mention any of these things to a complete stranger. You would delete, distort and generalise information so that the lost soul could understand you and find their way to the supermarket.

Here is another example of how we change information so that we understand it and so that it matches the way we want to see the world. I rarely go to public houses and so I do not notice them as I pass in my car. However, if I ask for directions, people often include all the public houses en route. As they travel the route in their minds, they are concentrating on the things that interest them.

Nominalisation

Clients will often describe an ongoing process (verb) as if it were a noun (name). They generalise and delete so much information that it is difficult for the coach to determine what exactly is being talked about. This is known as a nominalisation in NLP terminology. Politicians use nominalisations all the time to avoid being tied down on policies. "Law and order," "education," "health" and "wealth" are all nominalisations. Companies often adopt nominalisations as company values when they choose words that they think their shareholders or customers would want to hear: "respect," "honesty," "diversity," "integrity" and "quality."

Clients will construct sentences according to their way of looking at the world and you can get a clearer picture by a closer investigation of their meanings. For example, if a client says, "The management doesn't like me," you need to extrapolate who exactly in the management doesn't like them, what they mean by "management" and what it is about your client that this managerial person doesn't like.

Unspecified Nouns

You are not invited to be pedantic and searching just for the sake of it. Your client could avoid identifying a specific person because they are behaving as a victim. Once a client in victim mode has to talk about the person or an action, then they have no more excuses for not dealing with the situation. This example shows the use of "unspecified nouns."

Always challenge your clients when they do not specify who or what they are talking about. You can spot unspecified nouns when clients use general words like, "they," "people," "management," "the department," "it" – or any description where you cannot identify an individual person or a specific action.

If, at the outset of coaching, you discussed your client–coach relationship and the methods to be used, these should have included agreement that you had consent to subsequently challenge the client if it was necessary to help them to achieve their objectives. If you did this, your client will accept your challenges even if they create a degree of discomfort.

You must get to the hidden person and the deleted detail in order to create the necessary changes. Continue to ask the questions "Who, specifically?" or "What, specifically?" until your client names the person or the actual position of that person. If they are not prepared to divulge this information you are both attempting to row upstream without oars.

Once you have identified the perpetrator, your client will be forced to deal with the situation as it is. They will have replaced their existing behaviour – whereby they use generalisation tactics on themselves to avoid the pain of dealing with a problem that they probably hope will simply "go away" – with a new, more appropriate pattern.

Coaching for results frequently means that you make your client feel uncomfortable. To make this easier you can put a frame around the challenge. Framing is described in Chapter Nine.

"Yes" Set

Here is a useful example of a "yes" set: "You remember we agreed that I might sometimes have to challenge you in order for you to achieve your dreams? You do still want to [state the main outcome], don't you? So may I challenge you?"

The use of a "yes" set will help you to get your client into the pattern of saying "yes" before you ask the final challenging question. Once your client has agreed to your asking difficult questions, you must immediately ask, "Who or what, specifically?" Once you have the details you can start to move your client towards their outcome. Notice that I used the word "dreams" instead of "outcomes" or "goals" to get their agreement to the challenge. Dreams are more emotionally charged than outcomes or goals and, as a coach, you should attach some passion to the discussion.

A client in this example has dissociated from the situation. Dissociation is easy to spot because the client uses unspecified nouns such as those listed above to avoid feeling the pain that they have attached to the name of the person concerned. Pain can be a strong catalyst for positive action, particularly if this client is also an "away-from" (see Chapter Fifteen, concerning Meta-programs).

The aim of this process is to get agreement for your challenge by using the "yes" set and then to get your client associated with the person or deed to evoke their passion for action.

Unspecified Verbs

Unspecified nouns can leave you asking "Who?" and "What?" but unspecified verbs need you to ask your clients, "How, specifically?" Verbs are action words and can easily be made or left vague within a sentence. When your clients use a verb but leave it unspecified by omitting any qualifying material to give the verb more meaning, you must recognise this and challenge them with a "How?"

For example a client may say, "I always go to Susan because she helps me." The trap for the coach is to assume that the help Susan gives will be the right help, the help that is needed and the help to benefit the client. Unfortunately, this is not always the case.

It is human nature to believe that because someone agrees with you they have your best interests at heart. I am sure you can see the hole in the logic of this. In the example, Susan may be the client's best friend and this would cloud her judgment. She may not even want your client to succeed for several reasons, not least being that, if your client succeeds, Susan may be left behind. Susan may feel that she has to do something she does not want to do, or, quite simply, she may be jealous of your client.

It is very important when the verb is not specified to ask the question, "How specifically does Susan help you?" You need to know a lot more about Susan – her relationship with your client, her values and beliefs, her skills and background, what she may be able to offer and, most significantly, what power of influence she can wield over your client. Susan can be great support for your client. Equally she can be a millstone around the client's neck. You must find out which she is and avoid making assumptions, which may cost you your client and any future referral business. If you discover that Susan is not going to be a support, then use all the techniques in this book to loosen the hold that she has over your client.

The process for dealing with unspecified verbs is to ask, "How, specifically?" so that you can avoid assumptions. You also need to know the details in order to move your clients towards their goals.

Modal Operators

In Chapter Thirteen we looked at modal operators of possibility and necessity and as a coach you need to understand that both need to be challenged. If you allow your clients to believe they are victims you are doing our life coaching profession a great disservice.

When clients use phrases such as "I must," "I ought to," "I should," "It is my duty," they are being a victim and are caught in a necessity mode. Ask, "What would happen if you did?" Wait for your client to answer. If they reply, "I don't know" ask, "If you did know, what do you think it might be?" As crazy as this may sound, it works. The success of this second question is accomplished because it takes away the pressure of commitment and allows the unconscious mind to relax and supply the answer.

If a client tells you, "I should work more closely with John," ask, "What would happen if you didn't work more closely with John?" Your client now has to explore what they are currently doing (not working closely with John) and what will be the effect of continuing with their current behaviour. This could be the first time that they have viewed the outcome of their actions from this perspective.

Clients working with a modal operator of possibility will present you with "I can" or "I can't do that" or any other phrase that restricts them from taking any action.

"I can" is great news for the coach, since it means that your client is open and ready to take action. The limiting-belief phrases "I can't" and "It's impossible" are important to watch for because they reinforce behaviours and indicate a solid state of being. This solid state is total and difficult for the coach to alter.

There are two means of challenge in this instance. The first one does not need any frame, just a simple question: "What would happen if you did?" or "What wouldn't happen if you didn't?" Sometimes you can ask both questions, one immediately after the other, to get your client really thinking. The second is to ask, "What's stopping you from ...?" Clients rarely review habitual states of inactivity and, by drawing their attention to this limiting way of thinking, you can help them grow.

The really hard-hitting way of dealing with "I can't" is to challenge your client with, "What you're really saying is, 'I won't,' that we both know that [the action under discussion] is possible to do, and that you can do it. You've probably done something similar in the past. By saying, 'I can't' you're actually choosing not to do it, aren't you?"

This approach demands a secure and excellent client–coach relationship and you must be in rapport before you challenge in this way because your challenge will instantly throw you out of rapport. Your client will be uncomfortable with this provocation and you may wish to frame it beforehand or to reframe as soon as your client has acknowledged their behaviour. This technique should be used only during a face-to-face coaching session where you can constantly monitor your client's body language. Despite these risks or limitations, the technique can yield outstanding results when it is correctly applied. You must also re-establish rapport before the session ends.

Comparisons and Judgments

There are two similar Meta-language patterns. "Comparisons" and "judgments" each have information missing and both need to be challenged. When a client states, "I've been lazy since our last session," you need to know what your client is comparing "lazy" with. Compared with my other clients? The client could not know this, so must be making assumptions.

Compared with their partner, the previous session with you, their boss or the milkman? Without the other side of their comparison, you could fall into the trap of assuming, so always ask, "Compared with whom?" or "Compared with what?" Many clients unrealistically compare themselves with superheroes or with impractical aims. You could use a reframe: "I had a client who always said that he'd been lazy, but still managed to accomplish one of the agreed tasks each session, so he was steadily moving forward, like the tortoise in the 'Hare and the Tortoise' fable."

Judgments are generally opinion-based. This means that you need to find out just whose opinion your client is using for the comparison. Clients can sometimes say, "I am stupid." Ask, "Who says that you're stupid?" It does not matter whether they say, "Harry Smith" or "I do", because your next and immediate question is, "What criteria did Harry [or you] use to determine this?"

When you contest a statement such as "I am stupid" your client may shrug or attempt to avoid discussing it by saying that they did not mean it. Continue to explore a little deeper and you may unblock a childhood belief. Remind your client that, even if they said they were stupid in jest, their unconscious mind will be listening along with their self-image and creating actions to support this statement.

When your client uses words like "obviously," "clearly" and "patently," they omit the person or persons making the judgment:

- "It is obvious that I won't get the promotion"
- "It is clearly too difficult for a woman to become a director"
- "Patently, my boss thinks I'm not worthy"
- "I must obviously join the directors' club"
- "Clearly, you cannot start a coaching practice without qualifications"

In each instance, the questions are: Who is behind these statements? What measures are being used? How up to date are these measures? It is obvious that you should always question these types of statement. Is it?

Mind Reading

Mind reading is an easy trap for both the unwary coach and the client. It is an assumption that you know, or that others know, what is going on in the mind. It can arise where we project our thoughts onto the client and vice versa. A client might say:

- "I know my manager thinks my report is crap"
- "Sam thinks I will never run a mile"
- "My mother is lonely"

- "You're the coach: you should know if I've done it or not"
- "You are just like me"
- "He should know I wanted the job"

How exactly do you know? Get your clients to explain the reasoning behind any mind-reading statements that they make.

CLIENT: He should know that I want the job.
COACH: How exactly should he know?
CLIENT: Because I always work late.

Complex Equivalence

The mind-reading statement has moved into what is known in NLP as a "complex equivalence." The client's logic is that "this means that," so, in the above example, "working late means that I want promotion." As a coach you can immediately see that there is no connection. The trick is to get your client to see it, too.

Ask, "I'm a bit confused. How exactly does working late mean that you want promotion?" You are forcing your client to consider the fact that the boss may not be a mind reader. Then, "So how can you let your boss know you want promotion?" Now you are looking for your client to say they will go and *tell* the boss they want promotion.

Do not let your client off the hook if they say, "I'll point out how much overtime I've been doing" or any similar avoidance tactics. You need commitment that the client will arrange a meeting with the boss to discuss the position, the desire for the job and what they need to do to be considered for the vacancy.

Another example of mind reading will require your extra care and attention. This is where clients believe that their partners should be mind readers.

CLIENT: She should know that I love her.
COACH: How exactly should she know?
CLIENT: Because I'm still married to her [or variations on this theme].

COACH: I'm a bit confused. How exactly does still being married to her mean that you love your wife?

When dealing with marital issues you must take care. Before asking for suggestions of behaviour changes, question your client to find out the background, the current situation and your client's goals within the relationship. Notice the words "asking for suggestions of behaviour changes." Your client is the only one with the information needed to propose a course of action for enhancing the relationship. First, you need to encourage your client actually to tell their partner they love them. Then encourage them to think of changes in habitual behaviours that can prevent further deterioration of the relationship.

Ask your client about activities that they enjoyed together at the beginning of their relationship. Ask about anything that their partner really enjoyed during the relationship. These questions generally generate the ideas and activities necessary for improving the relationship. Take these ideas and ask your client to put them in order of priority. For instance, consider:

- the impact on their partner
- whether the ideas are achievable
- what the associated costs are
- what available time there is
- the ideal timing and your client's desire to do it

Suggest that they use a matrix similar to the example in Chapter Six. They should change the headings to suit this situation but keep the number allocations.

Universal Quantifiers

Universal quantifiers are another Meta-model distinction, and they can present themselves as limiting generalisations.

- "Jobs are hard to find"
- "Exercise is a waste of time"
- "Directors are pompous"
- "Wealthy people are crooks"

- "Only slim people are attractive"
- "It's who you know, not what you know"

These will all limit your client because the statements do not allow for any exceptions to the rule. Interestingly, we use universal quantifiers without considering the limiting consequences. One of the methods of drawing attention to the lack of flexibility in the statement is to embellish and amplify it until your client can see how ridiculous it is. "You're right. Only slim people get married, only slim people get on television, only slim people have sex." Eventually your client will see how foolish the statement is.

Another method of dealing with universal quantifiers is to ask, "Has there ever been an honest wealthy person?" By asking, "Has there ever been …?" you make your client consider how ludicrous their generalisations are.

If clients use "everyone," "always," "never," "nobody," they are generalising with a limitation and therefore using universal quantifiers. A quick challenge to the use of "everyone" etc. is to repeat the word as a question: "Everyone?" "Always?" "Never?" "Nobody?"

Dealing with universal quantifiers is always easy. Every coach knows you can exaggerate the generalisation used by your client, or you can question the validity of the statement made by your client.

Cause and Effect

The concept of cause and effect is easily described with "this means that."

- "I would go to the gym but I don't have time"
- "I'm happy now that Jack's left home"
- "She made me angry"
- "I would walk but it's dangerous around here"
- "I would lose weight if I could find someone to go to the classes with me"

The client is linking one thing with another and, on some occasions, this linking allows the client to blame other people for their emotional state. See Chapter Ten, which will give you some insight to state control. Cause and effect are often indicated when your client uses "but," followed by an excuse for not doing something.

Help your client to dissociate one thing from another by using questions such as "How does this cause that exactly?", "What has to happen for this not to cause that?" and "How do you make yourself feel like this?"

Clients who presuppose can be making assumptions that limit them. You can challenge this limitation. Some presuppositions are connected with a cause-and-effect statement:

- "When I get this job I'll be respected" (client is not respected now)
- "I'll work hard on these tasks" (the agreed tasks are difficult)
- "When I get fit" (your client is not fit now)
- "Since I moved house I've had nothing but bad luck" (the house is bad luck)

Ask your client why they believe what they are saying and what led them to this belief.

Presuppositions

Presuppositions can be a great coaching tool and you can use them to get your client to do tasks by presupposing yourself. Here are some suggestions:

- "When would be a good time to start the slimming classes?" (client will start)
- "Which task would you like to do first?" (client will do all the tasks)
- "Would you like to start the next session at the same time?" (client is going to rebook coaching with you)
- "How often do you want the coaching: weekly or fortnightly?" (client wants coaching)
- "How easy did you find that?" (it was easy)

- "Will you write the proposal today or tomorrow?" (the proposal will be written)
- "How many times will you visit the gym?" (client will visit the gym)
- "What will you replace biscuits with?" (client will replace biscuits)
- "Which is more important to you: X or Y?" (both X and Y are important)
- "Which day of the week is best for sending out mail shots?" (client will send out mail shots)

If you think about what you want your clients to achieve and presuppose that they will do it, you have them in the presupposition web. Clients can find it hard to challenge you but, if they do, this will give you extra information about their attitude to the task.

Embedded Commands

Now, when you use presupposition with an embedded command within the sentence, you will achieve effective results. That sentence has a presupposition and an embedded command.

Now, when you *use* presupposition with an embedded command within the sentence, you *will* achieve effective results. The presupposition is that you *will* achieve effective results and the embedded command is to *use* them *now*. One of my coaches, Sofia Pallesen, used a really great presupposition with an embedded command, "When would now be a good time to start?"

The presupposition was that I would *start*, and that *now is a good time*; the embedded command was that I would start now. I was so impressed that I immediately told Sofia that I would like to share this with you in this book, and she agreed.

Meta-language is about being exact, challenging your clients when they are not being precise or are being vague. When you use Meta-language patterns you can improve your effective coaching skills.

Summary

- Meta-language patterns are precise and utilise the strengths and weaknesses of language
- Companies often adopt nominalisations as their company values
- "When would now be a good time to start?"
- Always challenge your clients when they do not specify who or what they are talking about
- "How easy is life coaching?" (life coaching is easy)

Chapter Fifteen

Coaching Meta-programs

'A Meta-program is your door to the world –
it is also the doorway to your brain'

Synopsis

There are different questions or techniques in identifying Meta-programs. Recognising the Meta-programs of your clients will help you to communicate more easily with them. It will help you to inspire and excite your clients to achieve their true potential. Leslie Cameron-Bandler identified about sixty different varieties of Meta-programs.

This chapter covers only those that are quick to identify and use. For ease and clarity, they have been described as types of client, which is not strictly true: they are temporary and contextual. Therefore they cannot be taken as definitive personality traits.

Meta-programs are most frequently found in Neuro-Linguistic Programming (NLP). They are contextual specific filters which we all use. Contextual means that they are neither definitive nor static. They change with the context or situation in which we find ourselves. In plain English, they are the ways that we see and interpret what goes on around us, and we do not use the same ones all of the time.

The author and researcher Leslie Cameron-Bandler (see Bibliography) identified about sixty different Meta-programs. Shelle Rose Charvet, in her book *Words That Change Minds*, likens a Meta-program to a door through which we interact with the world. This door has a particular shape and has the power to select the information that we allow to enter the brain.

All your clients will be using their own Meta-programs and an understanding of these will enable you to help them achieve their goals. I have used my Meta-programs in selecting the examples to include in this book.

For ease and clarity, I have chosen to describe Meta-programs as types of clients. This is not a true definition because they do not reflect definitive personality types. But, in a coaching environment, this basic understanding will help you. Get it right and you will establish excellent rapport. Conversely, if you get it wrong, you may lose clients. A key point to remember is that all Meta-programs are grouped in opposing pairs.

Sameness and Difference

"Sameness clients" like the world to remain the same. "Difference clients" want the world to change constantly and be different. When opening coaching conversations, you must include both sameness and difference phrases.

For example: "Some of the goals will be the same as those that you've worked on before. We'll also be looking at different ways to achieve them." When you include both words in your opening sentences, you will be assured of arousing their interest, regardless of their preferred viewpoint.

You can recognise sameness or difference by asking about the relationship between their holidays of this year and last year. Sameness clients are inclined to say that it was the same place or same country. Maybe even the same airline. Difference clients would say it was different, a completely different destination, different friends and a different time of the year.

This relationship-and-comparing method is a quick and easy way of distinguishing between the two Meta-programs. You can replace the word "holiday" with a more appropriate choice that is relevant to the discussion. For instance, considering their job, home or car will give you the information that you require to find the distinction.

When dealing with sameness clients, fill your language and your proposals with things that are the same or similar to what they already understand. Always look for events or things that can be compared to past experiences that they can identify with. When your sameness clients are nervous about achieving new goals, assure them of the safety aspect by comparing this event to a previous event that went well, then show how the two events are essentially the same.

When dealing with difference clients, fill your language and proposals with things that are different from their previous experience. Always look for events or things that have variety, and point out how each event and outcome will differ from those previously encountered.

There are two further subgroups under sameness and difference. These need not be explored here, because using both words during your coaching sessions will include clients in these subgroups.

Towards and Away

We have already seen brief references to "towards" and "away-from" clients. Towards clients are goal-motivated: they like to achieve, attain and prioritise. They may have trouble recognising problems or situations that they should avoid. Away-from clients recognise all too well what should be avoided. They are motivated by problems. They want to get away from problematic situations. They usually respond to negative situations and they have dilemmas working with priorities. To identify whether a client is a towards or away-from person, ask, "What do you want from your coaching sessions?"

Towards clients will talk about wanting to gain things or to achieve and move forward. They will have a list of things to do and are animated and excited about the prospect of a new challenge. Your job is to guide and support them. They will be so focused on the future and its rewards that they may not consider areas that could cause them to fail. It is important with these clients to expose all the pitfalls and to discuss them. Do not be alarmed if they are resistant to this discussion. It is paramount for you to address these areas in order to guarantee their desired outcomes. Failing to hold this type of discussion can lead to unattained goals for your clients.

Away-from clients want to move away from their current job, partner, life and problems. They will not be inspired or motivated by thoughts of change. As you focus on their desired goals, emphasise how they will be leaving behind, be removed from or distanced from their troublesome issues. Show how they can easily get away from their painful situation. Support them by continuously reinforcing the benefits of leaving behind their troubles.

Global and Specific

You can compare this Meta-program to a forest and its trees. What size information does your client like to receive? Does your client like the global big picture (the forest) or specific details (the trees)? "Global" clients want overviews, concepts and abstracts. "Specific" clients like to deal with sequences in a step-by-step format and they need to know every small detail.

To recognise the difference between global and specific, simply ask any open question and listen for the reply. Your specific clients will respond by giving you lots of details, and your global clients will respond with a very short, focused answer.

At the beginning of the coaching sessions, tell your clients that you will explain the overall aims and objectives, followed by the details of each session. The overall aims will appeal to your global clients and the details will involve your specific clients. You need to include both the big picture and the details in your first contact session.

At the end of this session, summarise and review where you have been. This will appeal to the specific clients. Finalise with overall aims, to bring back the attention of your global clients. If, during your first session, a client demonstrates restlessness, this indicates a possible global preference. Global clients are easily bored with detailed information. Change tactics and ask them to summarise. They will be quick, succinct and happy.

Give your global clients the big picture. They will jump from topic to topic during a coaching session so you just jump with them. One of your challenges will be ensuring clarity of the agreed results. Ask your global clients what they have agreed and they will recount the goals in a random format. You must concentrate, for it is at this stage that they will miss the important, difficult or complex goals that are essential for progress. They don't relish the thought of the work involved.

When dealing with specific clients you must work "by the book." Proceed in a sequential manner and do not move on until you get agreement. They will be uncomfortable if you talk randomly around subjects. They need to know exactly what is expected, in exactly the right order and in exactly the right measures. Make sure you summarise in the correct order and do not add any extra goals at this stage. Give them an array of facts, figures and finite details. If you are a global coach this may be a challenge for you.

Options and Procedures

"Options" clients like unlimited options, possibilities and choices. "Procedure" clients need to follow the rules, regulations and a step-by-step process. Ask, "What were the reasons for choosing your current job?" Options clients will give you lists of opportunities for promotion and possibilities for expansion and say that the work looked interesting or challenging. Procedure clients will tell you that they had no choice and then tell you the events, in sequential order, that led to their securing the job.

To inspire your options clients, frequently ask them to look for other alternatives, or other possibilities. They will be heartened and excited about the endless opportunities available. Your challenge is to get them to settle on the best. Options clients will be impressed if you "break the rules." This can be achieved by saying that you normally allow your clients one main aim but, in this special case, they can have two main aims. Always obtain agreement and commitment to the fulfilment of both aims. Options clients will rush to reassure you and they will be very appreciative.

There are two effective techniques to inspire procedure clients. The first is to say that you coach using only the official tried-and-tested method. If you belong to any recognised coaching organisations, institutions or committees, tell them about it. They will be happy to follow procedures that have been tried, tested or proved.

The second technique involves getting your procedure clients to start on the path of action quickly. Once they have started, reveal that there are several stages that must be accomplished in a certain order. Once they have started, procedure clients will be compelled to finish and to complete the procedure.

It is beneficial for you to recognise your own Meta-program preferences, as this knowledge will help you to build relationships with your clients. You will be able to compensate when you are coaching a client from a different Meta-program. If your own Meta-program is options, and your client has a procedures preference, you will be able to adjust your coaching by reducing the alternatives that you offer to this client while becoming more directive in your coaching style.

Summary

- Meta-programs are filters of information
- The Meta-programs covered in this chapter represent only a small section of the identified Meta-programs
- You can use Meta-programs to inspire, excite and motivate your clients
- Using the wrong Meta-program with a client could result in your losing that client
- Incorporating both opposing paired Meta-programs during your first session will improve communication, understanding, rapport and the probability of great outcomes

Chapter Sixteen

Metaphors with Meaning

'Metaphors can enable or disable. Either way,
they are powerful catalysts for change'

Synopsis

In Neuro-Linguistic Programming (NLP), the word "metaphor" incorporates long or short stories, allegories, parables, similes, poems, jokes and quotes. Your clients already use metaphors to describe the way they perceive their lives. In order to get fast results, reorganise your clients' metaphor language. You can change their metaphors or use alternative metaphors to give them choice of action to help them achieve their outcomes.

Reading this chapter is like entering an Aladdin's cave – full of wonderment, curiosity, excitement and anticipation. Just like the day twenty years ago when I was strolling along the beach listening to the gentle swishing of the tide on the sand. I noticed an old man with grey hair, wearing a silver cloak and sitting on a rock. He beckoned me to sit beside him and after many hours together he told me that he knew the secret of wealth. The secret, if practised continuously, would fill my life with richness for ever. Over many months he painstakingly revealed his secret to me. I shall always be indebted to that old man. This chapter holds the secret, told to me all those years ago by the old man on the rock. Read on and discover the secret for yourself.

Metaphor in the world of Neuro-Linguistic Programming (NLP) is not confined to being a figure of speech: it is a general description of many things and that is why being able, as a life coach, to use a metaphor is very important. Think of a metaphor as being like a patchwork quilt, full of different forms of language and having the ability to offer a choice of meanings. The metaphor quilt is made of patches of long or short stories, allegories, parables, similes, poems, jokes and quotations. Metaphors offer choices for you and your clients. They can open up different ways of approaching problems and guide clients to discover resources within themselves. Your imagination and creativity are the only limits to your metaphor skill.

Clients use metaphors all the time when describing their lives. For example one client may say, "Life is an uphill struggle." Another probably says, " Life is a breeze." What information does this give you? Think about it for a moment.

"Life is an uphill struggle." What could this metaphor tell us about clients? Are their lives always an uphill struggle or is it just that today seems an uphill struggle? Are they viewing the current problem as being their whole life rather than a single event? Perhaps they are only looking for a feeling of significance by using dramatisation? What kind of outlook on life could a person have if they used this metaphor daily? How could you help them change that?

This pattern of speech is continually controlling results for this client. It is your role to change a poor pattern and to offer alternatives which enable them to achieve a more balanced outlook on life.

Asking questions about a client's metaphors will help to reveal any underlying meanings. In the above example, you could simply ask, "How big is the hill?" This will break the negative pattern of thinking and give you the opportunity to offer different choices. This "thinking-pattern interrupt" will also give your client the chance to consider the fact that all hills have peaks and therefore there is always an end or peak to all difficulties.

Alternatively, you could offer, "I've always found that, even if sometimes it take a little effort to climb a hill, the reward is always exhilarating. Once I've reached the top, the feelings of success are euphoric and the views are wonderful. Can you remember a time you reached the top of a hill and found a beautiful view?" You have now associated "uphill struggle" with the idea of reaching a "beautiful view" or "reward."

Another way of dealing with this metaphor is to ask the question, "What will the view look like when you've reached the top of this hill?" If they respond by saying that they have no idea, ask them, "If you could imagine the view, what would that be like? Clients nearly always have an answer and, usually, it is stated in positive terms.

However, if their answer is very bleak or negative you now have a choice. Continue to change metaphors until your client transforms. If all approaches draw a blank, gently suggest that they consider consulting a therapist. It is your call. You decide whether you have the skills to deal with this or whether, in your opinion, the problem requires the professional attention of a therapist.

"Life is a breeze." What could this metaphor tell us about clients? It could mean that they sail (notice my metaphor) through life dealing with challenges easily and effectively. It could mean that they ignore the challenges or problems by not acknowledging them, and therefore not finding a resolution.

If they mean "life is a breeze" today, ask: "How strong is the breeze and is it probable that the force of the breeze will increase?" Their answer may give you some insight about your client's motivation and method of working.

"What direction is the breeze heading?" may reveal that the breeze is blowing your clients towards the cliffs and imminent disaster. Conversely the answer may reveal subconsciously hidden goals or desires that your clients were unaware of. In either case you will discover some valuable information to help you coach them.

Listen constantly for any metaphors that disable your clients and replace them with metaphors that will enable them to reach their goals. Removing or altering negative metaphors changes their power over the client, thus shifting another obstacle from their pathway of success.

Films offer great metaphors that you can use as catalysts for client change. This is especially effective with clients who use metaphors frequently when they describe their situation. These clients are usually very susceptible to metaphorical suggestions. This makes it much easier for you to help them.

When a client uses a metaphor such as "Life is like a battle [or struggle or war]," I may replace it with a well-known quotation from the Paramount movie *Forrest Gump* starring Tom Hanks. You may already know it. "Life is like a box of chocolates: you never know what you're gonna get." This little aphorism offers your clients more than chocolates: it offers choices.

One of my clients retorted that he always picked the chocolates he did not like. To alter this pattern I reminded him that there are shops where you can choose which chocolates are put into the box. He could therefore fill his box with the kind that he liked. It was like hearing a penny drop (another metaphor). After a pause he said, "Yes I *can* do that, can't I?"

He had trapped himself in a loop of poor metaphors. By changing the old metaphor to "Life is like a sweet shop and I am the shop-keeper," he changed his view of life and has since started his own business and now enjoys a challenge.

Sometimes I use a short story that I have adapted from *A 2nd Helping of Chicken Soup for the Soul*, by Jack Canfield and Mark Victor Hansen.

One day, in the heat of June, a group of men were in the fields gathering the harvest. They had risen with the sun and laboured hard all day long. None had eaten since the previous evening and a massive hunger was upon them. As dusk was descending they began describing all the foods they would be eating and how big their feasts would be.

Among them one young man said nothing. Eventually the harvesters asked if his silence meant that he was not hungry. He smiled and nodded that he was not hungry. After several more hours of labour they all sat down to eat. The young man piled his plate higher than the others and started eating with great zeal. They all looked at him in amazement and reminded that him that not so long ago he said he was not hungry. He smiled and said that it was not wise to be hungry when there was no food around.

I use this metaphor with clients who lament that they do not possess something. Although it is futile to second-guess the interpretation that clients may take from this metaphor, I aim to achieve three things. The first and most obvious is that clients are wasting their time talking about things they currently do not have, unless, they are talking about planning to achieve these things. The second is the subconscious message that they will eventually get "it" – just as the food came to the young man. Finally, when they do get "it" they will enjoy "it" just as much, even if they do not participate in any futile chatter.

So, what are the metaphors that your clients are using? Do they enable or disable your clients? Do you need to intervene and change them? Do you need to offer alternative metaphors? Deal with one area or aspect at a time. Seamlessly and smoothly change or substitute metaphors to enable clients and provide choices of action.

You can create metaphors from the events in your own life or from the lives of others. Clients will not dispute something that has happened to you or to someone else. One of my clients wanted to lose weight and decided that she would start by giving up biscuits.

I said, "I had a friend who believed that giving up food was the best way to lose weight. She always found that after losing weight she would regain it within a short time. Then she changed her approach. Instead of giving up biscuits she decided to replace them with fruit. This allowed her to give herself a treat and not deprive herself of something. Whenever she replaced sweet foods with fruits she would congratulate herself for being kind to her body and for giving herself a healthy energy boost.

"She lost over thirteen kilos with this one small dietary change and, to my knowledge, has never regained the weight. At first she replaced only biscuits with fruit but, once the taste of success was on her lips, she began replacing other sweet foods. Now she does not eat any food containing refined sugars."

This metaphor is simple, indisputable and based on everyday life. Notice I used the words "small dietary change," to present the change as insignificant and easy to do. I selected the words carefully to reduce resistance to change. There is an unlimited supply of metaphors you can narrate to your clients. Remember that the metaphors do not have to be real. They must have your client's best interest in mind.

Whenever you relate a metaphor, remember that you will also be listening and consequently you will also benefit in the telling. Make your metaphors effective, fun, interesting and powerful and you will inspire yourself and your clients.

Metaphors can include words from familiar songs, poems, quotations or any source of inspiration, which will help you to achieve your client's outcomes. You do not need to be an author to use them.

Do metaphors work? The story that opened this chapter has brought you this far. So the answer to that is undeniable; they do.

Summary

- Metaphors in NLP encompass several areas of language
- Changing a metaphor can give your clients choices of action that they had not previously considered
- Phrases from songs or quotes from films are great tools in the world of metaphor intervention
- You do not have to be an author to write a metaphor

Chapter Seventeen

The Spiral Coaching Model

'There is a map, a pathway and a staircase of human evolution,
but the staircase is a spiral'

Synopsis

There is significant research to show that the way you see the world goes hand in hand with your beliefs and values. The Spiral Coaching model provides information to enable you to know which coaching approach will work – where, when and with whom. You will be able to coach someone who thinks about things and situations from a completely different viewpoint.

The Spiral Coaching model is founded on research started over forty years ago by Dr Clare W. Graves, a professor of psychology working in the United States after the Second World War. Don Edward Beck and Christopher C. Cowan, who co-authored the book *Spiral Dynamics: Mastering Values, Leadership, and Change*, continued and expanded it.

Steve Creffield's article "The Spiral Staircase" was the inspiration for the Spiral Coaching model. Only six of the colour-coded landings of the staircase are referred to, as these are the thinking patterns of those who are more inclined to hire your services.

Take your mind back ten years. How does your view of the world then, compare to or contrast with the way that you see it now?

That old view was formed by a certain set of beliefs and values. Today those beliefs and values may have changed and adapted synergistically with your lifestyle. They shape the way you see the world, but the way you see the world informs and shapes your values and beliefs.

Think about your coaching techniques and consider the impact of this reflexive loop. Ten years ago a particular coaching approach would have been appropriate for you. It would fit those old beliefs and values. Now, a decade later, you will doubtless require a different approach.

There is a map, a pathway, and a staircase of human evolution. It helps you to know what coaching approach will work where, when and with whom. You will be able to coach someone who shares your values and beliefs today. You will also be able to coach clients who differ from you considerably – perhaps someone who holds the very same values and beliefs that you held ten years ago!

There is a critically important principle here. Understand it and you will learn how to coach someone so that you connect everything you do to their natural motivational tendencies. It is much easier to work with their current way of seeing the world than it is to attempt to change it. I have noticed that some coaches become increasingly frustrated or disillusioned with clients who do not share their own beliefs and values. Yet it is the job of an effective coach to enter the world of the client and coach from there.

This chapter introduces a theory that will help you to enter that client world and connect your coaching techniques to their prevailing individual beliefs and values.

The Spiral Coaching model is based on research begun over forty years ago by Clare W. Graves, a professor of psychology working in the United States after the Second World War. Graves was fed up with trying to justify to his students the conflicting views of eminent psychologists. Had one of them got it wrong? This started his quest to find out what makes us behave differently and what makes some adapt and change while others, in the same situation, remain constant.

He concluded that we change and adapt according to the conditions in which we live. Over time he could see a pattern emerging. This pattern clearly showed that the human mind evolves in a particular way, and along a particular trajectory.

In a 1999 article, "The Spiral Staircase," the author Steve Creffield likened this trajectory to a spiral staircase with an infinite number of stairs and clearly identifiable landings. His adaptation of Graves's theory suggests that anyone standing on a different landing from you may appear to be crazy, pathetic or evil in your perceptions. As a coach you could be tempted to change, reject or even rescue clients, instead of working with their thinking model and offering solutions that fit them.

Each landing on this spiral staircase is colour-coded with its related thinking patterns. These offer an insight into the different ways of thinking with specific coaching tips for each colour. You will discover why certain approaches do not work with individual clients and, more importantly, why others will succeed.

When you establish your client's colour, you can apply appropriate coaching interventions that fit and work with their natural thinking patterns and motivational tendencies. Simply ask, "What is important to you about life?" or "What do you think about this?" This will help you to determine the predominant colour code that is being presented.

It is important to understand that the colours do not define personality types. They are simply codes for different types of thinking patterns. As clients evolve to each colour level within the spiral, their level of thinking related to that colour will remain as a potential. So let us consider each of the six selected colour codes in turn.

Purple

To identify purple-thinking clients, look for examples of the rites of passage, rituals, symbols, traditions and metaphors. This pattern is full of mysticism, custom, rituals, and close-knit clans or extended families. These clients are strongly influenced by mysticism and fate.

They will most probably consult with tarot or palm readers. Your help must be presented to achieve change without demeaning psychic healers or readers. Such clients may become victims of a dependence upon "psychic hotlines" or "horoscope phone lines," which could drain their cash resources. Resultant financial chaos could be the reason that they seek your help.

Purple-thinking clients may appear to be dominated by one person – a "chieftain" figure, who may be a partner, a boss, a parent or some other controlling figure in their life. Stories and metaphors easily influence them because these "old ways" are the preferred methods, which they use to train their offspring.

Use this knowledge to advantage. Make up stories; reframe bad events into opportunities for growth or potential areas of development. If you believe you are not good at constructing stories or myths, do some research. Go to your local library for inspiration. Short stories are a great place to start.

Within a commercial context, purple-thinkers will not be motivated by the normal means of annual rises, benefits or rewards given to individuals who outperform the team. They like to work as a team member and do not take kindly to incentives that promote disharmony. They will support, guide and be perfect advocates for team working.

Purple-thinkers record or measure time differently from most. They do it by using their kinaesthetic senses. They may have difficulty with timekeeping because they work with events in sequences rather than by conventional clocks. Their fluid approach to time can baffle them when anyone becomes outraged that they are late for, or totally miss, appointments.

You will need to establish some time-based ground rules for these clients. Always make it clear to them that missed appointments have to be paid for and you are not available at unallocated times for coaching sessions.

Ask them what they "feel" are the best routes or solutions to take or make and you will be almost sure to help them solve their problem. On most occasions, what they intuit will be the right decision for them. Have faith, even if you cannot always fathom the reasons behind their thoughts, as they have an enigmatic awareness of cause and effect.

Purple-thinking clients may quickly put the coach in the role of chieftain. You may be expected to fulfil the role of an adviser rather than a coach. Too much questioning during coaching may actually diminish your influence. They have come to you because they want to be led. Because they lack initiative they could be looking for you to manage or direct them.

They have great talents and strengths and will often be found in the arts or music. Any profession that permits expression of their natural creativity will be a great platform for success measured in their terms.

Purple-thinkers find it very difficult to deal with sudden changes to their lifestyle and you can help them to develop and cope with this. Sometimes, their association with you will bring about change events, thus perpetuating their need for you. Exploiting this need is unethical and you should take great care not to fall into this dangerous trap.

Red

The red-thinking client is a warrior or predator. These distinctions are found equally in men and women and lead your clients to a life addicted to instant pleasure. Clients operating from this view will seek pleasure at all costs. They get a buzz from sex, power, domination and control over others. It is this desire for "immediate gratification" without guilt that is the driving force behind their behaviour.

They want rewards now. It is important to show them how this can be achieved, and achieved quickly. When they report back to you that they have completed a goal, reward them immediately, right there and then.

In business, red-thinkers thrive on and understand a vertical hierarchy. It is in this environment that they build their own empires. They demand respect, results and compliance with their will. When results are not forthcoming, or mistakes are made, you can forget oral, written or final warnings. They will sack the offender on the spot, often in front of all the other employees.

Red-thinkers can be very creative, bringing energy and imagination to any company. They are fun-loving, free from normal constraints and can create product innovations, unique problem-solving solutions and dynamism. In the start-up years, it is often elements of the red-thinking mind that initiates the business and provides the drive and energy needed for success.

This is their healthy side. When their energy is captured, directed, focused and given clear boundaries it can exceed all expectations, break world records, turn a business around, bring products to market and break new ground in the shortest possible time. They will be looking for you to confirm the successes of their life.

They see charm as a weapon, not as a compliment. Red-thinkers use charm as warriors wield a sword, using it to get what they want, when they want it. Respect, power and dominance are their only measurable values of richness. You will have to appeal to immediate rewards in the goal-setting process. Long-term goals are not for the red-thinkers. The goal has to be macho, sexy and hard-hitting, and give them respect.

They are generally unwilling to plan. You need to do the planning with them and then direct each task as an order to be completed within a certain time frame. If they fail to complete the task you need to come down hard on them, along the lines of unfulfilled promises and assert your rights as coach in an unquestionable manner. Red-thinking clients will respect this and respond well. A common trait is their failure to save or organise their own finance. You need to understand that you cannot control their urges to spend. You can support red-thinkers only as far as they allow you to do so. When coaching red-thinkers, you will often hear them say, "It's not my fault," because they do not accept responsibility for failure. It is a waste of your time trying to show that it is OK to fail. They expect you to show them how to get out of the mess and make them look good.

Their relaxation may often take the form of contact sports. Their favourite films will include the *Rocky* series, *The Terminator*, *Die Hard* and any others with violence and heroism. Their relaxation is not about classical music and dinner for two: they prefer fast, furious fun.

Red-thinkers will call in debts of all kinds, as and when they feel it will be to their benefit. This is true of any debts that they believe you to owe them. Be warned that if you allow a red-thinker to introduce you to someone who can help you, a reward will be expected. Payment is not usually discussed before the introduction, so you will have no idea what your costs will be. Avoid becoming committed until you know the price you will pay.

Red-thinkers like to flaunt their power and dominant status. When coaching them, you can take many lessons from blue-thinkers (see below), as this is their next evolutionary landing on the spiral staircase. If you can coach your client to integrate, or at least work closely with someone who operates from the very best of blue thinking, you can enjoy watching your client stepping on to a whole new wave of success.

Red-thinkers are a challenge to coach. We all have red elements within us and sometimes it is hard not to judge their behaviours. With a red-thinking client, you must be hard-hitting and dominant. Be crystal clear about boundaries, goals and expectations and do not be afraid of delivering these messages explicitly. Never become indebted to them, as you will not know what price you will have to pay until it is too late. A red-thinker does not suffer from guilt and lives just for today and for today's rewards.

Blue

Your blue-thinking clients believe there is only one right way to live and it is their way: their religion, faith, rules, regulations, procedures, dress codes, social positions, grading and rankings. When dealing with blue-thinking clients, it is better to avoid discussions about right and wrong and concentrate on outcomes. Allow them to dictate the methods or procedures for attaining their outcomes.

The blue-thinker is a strong believer in what can and what cannot be done. It is futile to attempt to persuade them that there are alternatives. To do so could lose them as a client.

These clients will not be looking for quick ways to secure themselves promotion. Their satisfaction comes only from striving to fulfil their duty. They love rules and regulations, hierarchies and honour, and will be found in professions that support these beliefs. The armed forces, police, Conservative Party, lawyers, Masonic lodges, Rotary Clubs and old boys' networks are attractive to blue-thinking individuals.

Encourage your blue-thinking clients to follow the rules and to find a mentor within their working hierarchy. This allows them to develop their potential and increase their profile while remaining within the social boundaries that they believe in and feel comfortable with.

They believe in self-sacrifice and will look to you to deliver punishment when they have not completed previously agreed tasks. Blue-thinking is full of guilt, so use this in coaching to make them feel guilty for not achieving or reaching the goals you previously determined. They understand guilt and expect to feel it.

They will be looking for a regular job with regular pay structures and graded positions. The employment package will have to offer a pension scheme, as a blue-thinker wants to sacrifice today for a glorious future. Support these clients with set rules. Explain that you have rules that you expect your clients to adhere to. Send them a document called, say, "Rules of Business for Clients" (see Chapters Seven and Eighteen).

Do not recommend environments where self-expression and freedom are the underpinning modus operandi as blue-thinkers will not settle or perform well there. Encouraging them to push for promotion will be one of your challenges because they believe that they should be thankful for what they already have.

When a blue-thinker comes to you looking for a new job, prepare a list of questions that they should ask at interviews and send it to them prior to the interviews. The questions should include confirmation of pension schemes available for employees, promotions for hard work, grading scales of pay, uniform and written contracts of employment. These clients trust the written word and will expect to sign a contract with you. They will fulfil every detail of the contract to the absolute letter. Get a lawyer to check your contract before you issue it for signature. If you have testimonials from clients in authority or public office send a copy along with copies of any training certificates you have been awarded and preferably your membership of a professionally recognised body.

Areas of recreation for blue-thinkers could include the scouts, guides, Salvation Army, Special Constabulary or any organisation where uniforms are worn and grades have to be obtained by hard work and dedication.

They love ostentation, splendour, ceremony and rituals with rites of passage. Your blue-thinking clients will be serious and formal, believing that there is only one right way to live and it is their way. They love to know exactly what is expected of them and will be drawn to professions with well-defined dress codes, rules and regulations.

You may be asking, "Why would a blue-thinker consult a coach?" Often they hire a coach because people at "this grade" or in "this profession" and at "this level" have life coaching as a privilege of rank. They cannot be seen not to have a life coach, since this might be interpreted as "not making the grade."

Orange

This is a slick, demanding, punchy type of thinking and you had better be ready. Orange-thinkers do well as dynamic sales people and revel in the glory of sales successes. They will strive to attend the "Top Sales Club" (or similar) and will always want to win the holidays, prizes and bonuses. Money, success and achievement are their buzzwords and they will expect you to display wealth before they will employ you as coach.

Orange-thinkers are assertive in business, and are tough negotiators with strong entrepreneurial spirits. They will come to a coach to increase their lead in the marketplace and will look to you for clever solutions that exploit the situations they present to you.

They are multitasking and will expect you to demand excessive quantities of goals from them and to reinforce the material benefits or profits of accomplishment. They are high achievers and, although they may not be well-read, they will know the titles and authors of popular business literature, self-help books and biographies of entrepreneurial leaders or achievers. If they are on the road frequently they will listen to high-energy, motivational tapes or CDs in their car. They do not tolerate fools so think carefully before you speak on any subject.

Orange-thinking is found in abundance in the financial markets, posturing with all the accoutrements of wealth such as champagne, caviar and "designer everything." Money and rare or expensive goods are their measures of success. They will purchase cars with names synonymous with power, victory, mastery and glory. To get these symbols of success, the orange-thinker is likely to suffer from ulcers, irritable bowel syndrome, heart problems and mental or physical fatigue.

They could sacrifice health for wealth and you need to be aware of this in order to deliver truly effective coaching for them. Learn what your client eats along with what exercise they take. To encourage increased exercise, quote from the biographies of very successful people who state that the benefits of exercise helped them to achieve their goals. Link exercising to success and wealth and this will give them the motivation to start a regime. Expand on the networking opportunities for them if they join an exclusive health club.

To alter unhealthy eating habits, recommend very expensive, trendy, health-conscious restaurants. Suggest they employ a dietician and chef. If you can, quote a famous person who has both of these and is healthy, and then you will have more credibility. Anthony Robbins, of Robbins Research International, is a good example of success and health who said he employs a chef to prepare his nutritional meals.

Orange-thinkers are stimulated by quick successes far more than by slower and longer-term goals. You will need to keep them focused on the current rewards while guiding them to long-term prosperity. They believe that anyone can achieve success if they put their minds to it and, therefore, they are often short on empathy for the underdog. They will experience great challenges in management positions because they can be derogatory and discriminating. As great believers in empowerment, they expect employees to have similar drives, ambitions and skills.

They are likely to become brusque if employees have difficulties and seek their help and guidance. They believe that their staff should be able to deal with any situations that arise. Encourage your orange-thinking clients to attend seminars on employment law, preferably delivered by lawyers who can demonstrate the downside of poor employee relationships and explain the harassment laws. This could be just enough to protect these clients from lawsuits.

During coaching sessions, orange-thinkers will be forthright if they feel that you are becoming boring and unfocused. They are easily distracted, so make sure that you have all their details to hand and that you efficiently dispense activities and rewards. Their attention span is limited to their interest in the topic or to impressing people who have something to offer and they will be dismissive as soon as they tire. Do not take this to heart – it is just the way that their minds work. Analyse the session and discover where you drifted off the point and make a note to be more focused next session. Orange-thinking clients can be demanding and may frequently identify areas of defect in your coaching sessions.

They always play to win and would rather lose a business deal on the golf course than come second. Their hobbies must have kudos and involve an elitist group. Sports such as squash, tennis, polo, show jumping and golf, where they can win and pose, will be attractive to them. Recommend that they join the best and most expensive clubs to demonstrate how well you understand them.

Orange-thinkers are more interested in the initial "chase and win," rather than the growth of love and companionship. They could easily marry for reasons of winning the position on the board as much as for winning the attention of the potential mate. They commit only when there is some real gain in terms of money or success. They may often be found in the divorce courts, where they will rarely come away as the loser.

Money, success and achievement are their buzzwords. You need to have glossy brochures, flashy cars and designer clothes. They will be impressed if you know someone rich and famous, and even more so if you have coached them.

Green

Your green-thinking client will want to work with you in a mutually beneficial way. They believe that everyone is dependent on everyone else, and that love, peace and harmony are the only true ways to live.

A green-thinker, working within a commercial corporation, may be balancing the need for income with the greed of commercialism and this could cause stress. If the organisation is serving some higher purpose or if they are within a team where all the members are consulted on everything, they will have a greater chance of career success. They could be found in companies similar to Anita Roddick's Body Shop, neatly combining commercialism with community values.

The green-thinker constantly wants to fit in and, when attending meetings in commercial organisations, is prone to accept untenable situations rather than disagree with others. They can be driven by a desire to feel part of the whole and they can suffer unsuitable working conditions. Rather than jeopardise the good feelings associated with fitting in, they are good at reducing group conflicts and help the team to reach agreements. Politically correct and fully versed with harassment and equality law, they are formidable if crossed and will not hesitate to point out the errors of any individual's ways, regardless of the position that they hold in the company.

Green-thinkers believe in the rights of the individual to have their voice heard. They are well suited to customer-care roles and any position within company call centres where they can help customers while also being part of a team. Environments where fair, defined rules and regulations are adhered to offer congenial working conditions for them. This situation will remove the burden of unfavourable decision making while providing a fair solution for the customer and perfect fairness for a green-thinker.

You may need to remind them of these excellent skills, as they are inclined to underrate their talents, believing that, because the skills come naturally to them, they are not of any great worth. Green-thinkers would work well in pre-sale roles where they can create a solid customer-focused relationship that will help secure the final sale.

A green-thinker is drawn to the caring professions, where they can use their finely-honed intuition and interpersonal skills. Green-thinking is common in counselling, therapy or life coaching. Are you on the green landing of the spiral? If the answer is yes, remember the challenges you will have when coaching red- or orange-thinking clients, and coach from their particular world view, not from your own.

Green-thinkers will not be coming to you for help in achieving huge financial gains. They may come to you when their company is undergoing a re-engineering process and redundancies are imminent.

In relationships, they will subdue their own desires in order to harmonise. They prefer to be liked and will sacrifice themselves for their partner. Some may select the underdog as a partner and will like to spend time and resources on them. As their coach, you may have to pick up the pieces after they have been taken for a fool – either as a partner or as a supporter of a losing cause.

Green-thinkers are often found doing voluntary work or joining protests. They will be supporters in any cause where the universe or any of its inhabitants are adversely affected. If you support any similar causes, be sure to let these clients know about it, as this will help to build trust and rapport.

Their clothes have to be comfortable and serviceable rather than glamorous and trendy. Appearance may be an area that has to be addressed by you, especially if your clients are attending inter-views with companies that have strict but unspoken dress codes. Diplomacy and tact will be needed to handle this sensitive area. Remind your clients of their original outcomes before broaching the subject. Revisit the reasons behind their applying for the posi-tion. This could lead you to recommend an appointment with an image consultant or to suggest that your client should review their outcomes in the light of the new circumstances.

If a green-thinking coach works with a red-thinking client, the coach will need to keep a firm check on the desire to judge actions. Such a client will shock and sometimes horrify them. Coaching from a purple or green background will be a significant challenge. A coach operating from these cooler colours may actually choose not to work with the red-thinking mindset, since such clients will disappoint their coach on more than one occasion.

However, green-thinking coaches are very often drawn to them, under the impression that they can rescue red-thinkers from their addictions, in the belief that something in their upbringing or life experiences have brought about such "inhumane" behaviour. In essence, the coach will attempt to lead them into green-thinking, a strategy that is doomed to failure. The red-thinker will have little respect for the coach, and would interpret green-thinking as weak. Red cunning and conniving can manipulate and exploit any empathic approach.

If you are coaching a blue-thinking client and you are a green-thinking coach, you may have a huge challenge exploiting this guilt aspect. If you became a coach to help other people achieve their goals, which I truly hope you did, you will find that effective coaching is achieved by working within your client's model of the world, not your own. Fully appreciate the drivers or catalysts for blue-thinkers and use them to move the client forward. A green-thinking coach does not respond well, unlike the blue-thinkers, to authority figures who trot out credentials so they need to keep a tight grip on their opinions and coach from competency within an open context.

Yellow

It is conceivable for a yellow-thinker to be your coach, as this colour code is on the second tier of the spiral model and incorporates the previous colours, this gives them more alternatives and a broader view of things. Yellow-thinkers may frequently come to you for short, focused coaching programmes. They will have a goal clearly defined and seek support and knowledge. This is the only colour where they will hire a coach entirely on the basis of the coach's knowledge and experience.

A yellow-thinker seeks information and could be well-read in a wide diversity of subjects. If you agree that reading a book is a task for this client, they will read all the available books on the selected subject. Knowledge is one of their main motivations. They seek knowledge for knowledge's sake and they will demand as much information, wisdom and knowledge as is possible. Yellow-thinkers are interested in learning and, even if they do not have several qualifications, they will be well educated. They have a talent for working on several levels and topics at one time and can adapt their learning style to speed up the process of information selection.

Your yellow-thinker is an independent client who is not bothered what other people think, although they will be interested in their ideas. This means that you can comfortably recommend that they should consult an expert in a certain field or speciality.

They will easily admit a need for others to help them achieve goals. In an environment where they are required to work with others, they will work as part of a team only to get the task completed. After the job has been done they will remove themselves before any praise, glory or honour is bestowed.

A yellow-thinker is happy to leave the acclaim for others to enjoy and does not need external appreciation. This may present a challenge for you, as praise is not a motivating factor for this client. They, however, will be content just to have succeeded in a task. Do not overemphasise your praise or congratulations. One of the best ways of dealing with successful completion of tasks is to say, "Only you know how well you have done" or "I'm sure that you're fully aware of how successful you've been."

Yellow thinking has a well-developed self-esteem founded on what they know rather than on any emotional ego. It is unassuming enough to acknowledge shortcomings and this may be the reason that they use your services. They will not apportion blame or carry guilt for lacking a skill that they need. They simply understand their own failings and forgive themselves.

The main aim for a yellow-thinker is personal freedom. They will, with your help, want to achieve this without harming others. This presents a challenge, because, at times, they can become ruthless if they feel that the situation calls for this approach.

They can be diplomatic if this means they will achieve their outcomes, or, conversely, they can be authoritarian should this be the best approach. They are a natural mix of contrasting viewpoints, so take care not to prejudge them as being contradictory, traitorous, untrustworthy or unreliable. They are committed to their own causes, which allows them to be flexible to achieve their goals.

Yellow-thinkers know that they need other people but they will not become emotionally dependent on you, their partners, and their spouses, any family member or friend. They need directed support or expertise from their coach and nothing more. Offer only what is asked, then they will think highly of you and recommend your services to all who they believe could benefit. Display unfounded or silly emotions and they will drop you like a hot cake.

Note

The Graves theory is only briefly introduced here. This chapter is my interpretation, based on the book *Spiral Dynamics: Mastering Values, Leadership, and Change* by Don Edward Beck and Christopher C. Cowan, adapted for use by life coaches. Their book is recommended as essential reading for every coach.

The colour coding suggested here is exactly the same as that used by Beck and Cowan. This is to enable you to compare and easily identify the route and inspiration of the coaching spiral. As a life coach, you will find that the benefits of understanding the whole system are far greater than those outlined here.

The concept can be used to find solutions for conflicts, business planning, business process engineering, training and personal development.

Summary

- Whenever the colours are mentioned, it does not mean types of people: it simply codes the types of thinking patterns that they adopt
- Purple-thinking is full of mystlcism, custom and rituals seeking safety in a mysterious world where reciprocity often rules
- The red-thinking client is a warrior or aggressor seeking power and control
- Blue-thinking clients believe there is only one right way seeking meaning and purpose in life
- Orange-thinking is slick, demanding and punchy, seeking influence and possibilities
- Green-thinking clients will want to work with you in a mutually beneficial way seeking peace of mind, dignity and plenty for all
- Yellow-thinkers seek short, sharp coaching programmes, seeking to understand complex, integrated living systems of which they are a part

Chapter Eighteen

The Secrets of Coaching Success

'The pipeline effect means that the delay between input and output is usually well worth the wait'

Synopsis

Starting a new practice may seem daunting but you do not have to change much in your current lifestyle. Market positioning requires that you seriously think about what markets you want to work in. At least 40 per cent of your working hours must be spent in growing your practice. Networking skills are essential.

If you send out a client code of conduct, consider tempering its impact with a "promise" document. The last coaching call is as important as the first. A referral system will be your primary source for clients. Training as a life coach is important.

You may need to set up bank accounts, VAT registration and data-protection registration and organise bookkeeping facilities. The future of life coaching cannot be predicted but I believe that there will always be a need for coaching in one form or another.

The biggest secret of coaching success is that there are no secrets. Life coaching is about the practical application of proven procedures with commitment. Although there are no trade secrets, there are several tips that established coaches have learned from hard work and experience. This chapter reveals these so that you can, for once, learn without having to follow the trial-and-error route for yourself.

Starting a new practice may seem a daunting prospect and, indeed, it is a big step into your future, but the really good news is that you do not have to change or vary your current lifestyle too much. Life coaching is one of the few professions that you can sample with minimum cost or risk before committing yourself fully. Then, by the time you want to commit, you will have already created a small practice. As long as you can allocate at least four hours each week, you can use them to dip your metaphoric toe in the rewarding water of life coaching.

Chapter Six explained that you require only four essential "props" to start your practice – a telephone, some notepaper or printed forms, a pen or pencil and a diary – and it described how you could generate initial leads through a simple marketing and referral system. Once you have started coaching, then all you have to do is to build your practice gradually and adopt some routines that will help to increase your client base.

Turning a part-time hobby into a fully profitable practice is not as hard as it may seem at first sight. You do require dedication, passion and commitment. The biggest requirement for inevitable success is the genuine desire to help other people in their own quest for success. It is strange that you need to make other people successful to become successful yourself and it is this paradox that first attracted me to the profession.

Unlike many other enterprises, your practice will enjoy profits in direct proportion to your effectiveness in helping other people to achieve success.

Market Positioning

Market positioning requires that you think seriously about the clients that you want to work with, where they are found and which demographic groups, trades or lifestyles you wish your practice to be aligned with. It is not merely chance that you have a life coaching *practice* and not a life coaching *business*. The word "practice" denotes that you have a profession rather than a trade. It is all about product positioning. Call your enterprise a business and you align yourself with wedding-cake makers, newsagents, garages and any other typical high-street business. Call your enterprise a practice and you align yourself with a completely different world.

Professionals run practices – and life coaching is a profession. Never give in to the temptation of demeaning your abilities and standards by using false modesty. Respect yourself and your talents at all times, and others will respect you as well.

Marketing your Practice

Marketing your practice means growing and expanding your client base. Professional marketing must be undertaken on a regular basis. You should allocate at least 40 per cent of your working week to the pursuit of growing your practice through public awareness and expanding your client base. You may hear this time called "producing a pipeline of prospects," because, as with oil flowing through an intercontinental pipeline, it takes time for your input – the promotion of your service – to arrive at the delivery point as the uptake of that service. The pipeline effect means that the delay between input and output is usually well worth the wait.

As an example of this, it has taken my own training company as long as three years in the corporate training arena to capture some of the contracts that we have pursued. The corporate world often issues three-yearly contracts for this type of service. To be even considered, it is necessary to produce a tender document months in advance. That stage may be reached only after many hours spent establishing and building a relationship with the potential purchaser. This can be equally true for public-sector coaching contracts so, if your plan includes penetration of the corporate or public marketplaces, take this pipeline effect into account when planning your budget and time.

You might choose to direct your marketing towards both the corporate and the private client. Targeting two separate groups doubles your chance of success. It also doubles your marketing workload, especially in the initial setup stages. The same marketing strategy and materials will not work for both of these very diverse markets.

If you are building your practice with very limited financial resources, then I suggest that you aim your marketing at the private sector of individual clients. The great advantage of this approach is that you can acquire clients simply by preparing a small home-printed brochure. The expense is tiny compared with the response that this can generate.

When you focus on this market you can use testimonials or client stories as part of your promotional information. The private individual is often attracted by a description of a personal experience when they would be bored by normal "marketing data." Ask your existing clients (even if, initially, you are practising on friends) to write a testimonial or a short story about their experiences as your client. If you are uncomfortable with this approach, surf the Internet and use the general quotes that feature in many coaching sites. Make sure you get written permission to use the quotes beforehand, so that you don't fall foul of copyright law.

The disadvantage of targeting private individuals is the existence of a "glass ceiling" to the upper level of the fees that you can charge. This limit is imposed by your potential clients' disposable income. If you have access to a circle of wealthy contacts, you can charge, and should charge, the standard corporate hourly fee. If, like most of us, you do not have access to the rich and famous, then you must adjust your fees accordingly. Take care not to destroy your credibility by going too low, however. Consider the potential value to the client rather than just your own time input. Once you have established a reputation in your chosen market, you can increase your fees accordingly.

Marketing to large companies requires a greater investment of time and money. You will need professionally designed and printed marketing materials along with top-quality printed business stationery. It can be difficult to penetrate this corporate sector without contacts or referrals, so be prepared to invest patience and persistence. The benefit of market penetration in this segment is in the fees that you can command once you have gained access. These will generally be at least three or four times the hourly rate that you can charge to an individual. The only limit on the fee is the corporate customer's perceived value of your service. Often, if you set your fees low, your tender will fail because there is a belief in the corporate marketplace that low prices equal low standards.

There is another important way of advancing your client numbers by positive marketing. Spend time listening to motivational tapes about marketing. The acknowledged master in this field is Jay Abraham. I strongly recommend that you listen to his highly original tapes or read his marketing books (see Bibliography).

Networking

Networking skills are essential to building your practice. It is well known among sales and marketing professionals that there is a direct relationship between your network of contacts and your sales figures. You need to spend some of your 40 per cent marketing time making contacts.

Listen to Anthony Robbins and any other great motivational speakers – either in person or through their extensive ranges of audiocassette programmes. One of the tips that I picked up from such tapes is that, to become a successful life coach, you must be interested in people to the extent that you want to know how you can help them increase their business and profits by your recommendation to business people whom you know.

The key to transcending difficulties in getting people interested in you is for you to become interested in them. When you use this tip, almost before you realise it, you will have a list of prospects and a pipeline of people wanting to be coached by you.

Growing Your Practice

Growing your practice should be constantly in your thoughts. Start by contacting local banks, building societies and accountancy practices and suggest offering your services to their clients. You can volunteer to speak at one of their regular meetings or contact them individually, starting with your own bank, building society and accountant. Your approach is to show them how, by making their clients more successful, it will, in turn, put more money into their pockets. Offering to give them a percentage of your coaching fee for each of their clients who engages your services may be the incentive that interests them the most.

With financial institutions, your leveraging point is that, when you coach their clients to reach their goals, any commitments that they have to the bank are more likely to be honoured promptly. When you coach an accountant's client you will be increasing the paid workload for that accountant, who will be able to pass on extra charges accordingly. So, when you offer a financial incentive and the added benefits of developing their clients, you should find eager cooperation for this informal form of liaison or partnership.

You can grow your practice by joining a business club. Some have monthly evening meetings with a speaker; some have regular dinner meetings; and there is a current vogue for clubs dedicated to holding business breakfasts. They all have a common denominator: to create a forum to network and promote their businesses. As a coach, you are ideally situated when you join one of these clubs because you can network for yourself and you can coach others to network.

It is surprisingly easy to become a committee member or even chairperson for one of these clubs, which is a great advantage when it comes to increasing your client base. Find and join your local group, even if "local" means travelling for thirty minutes or more to attend. These clubs are specially designed to promote business, so where better to be a member and promote your practice?

Closing a Sale

Sales-closing skills can often be overlooked or assumed, but you need to be confident that, having explained about your service and aroused interest, you can then secure the engagement. There is a four-step method for getting clients to employ your services. This is the method that my manager taught me several years ago, during my time as an account manager for a global IT manufacturer. I have slightly adapted it for its application in a life coaching practice.

It comes into play when you have completed the I for "interest" in the RABIT model (See Chapter Six) and you move on to "time" to close. As an alternative to the close mentioned earlier, try this approach:

"So now can you can see [or hear or feel – select your prospect's representational system as described in Chapter Eleven] how this would really help you to accomplish [the client's goals, which you will know by now]?"

"Do you want [client's goals as above]?"

"If you were going to hire a life coach, when would now be a good time?"

"I have a free session on Monday or Thursday – which will suit you better? ("Alternative" close technique.)

I have added in some embedded commands (see Chapter Fourteen) to add extra leverage to the model, which will increase your success rate. A high percentage of prospective clients will want to go ahead and book your services after this powerful close.

Once you have gained a client, the life-story technique bonds the relationship between you both. This involves asking your client to write their life story and to highlight the major life-shaping events that occurred. If your client becomes stuck or cannot remember, just recommend that they (where applicable) ask family members or old school friends for their input. Frame this by pointing out that family members and friends will always remember events according to their own model of the world and therefore it will, by the nature of things, be a distorted record. Your client should send you a copy of their story.

As a result of this exercise, clients often reveal their hidden talents, their forgotten dreams, goals and aims, and then discover that they overlooked their ability to be confident because of the general activity of living. This exercise can give your clients fresh or recycled ideas and new directions that will inspire them to greater accomplishment. It often renews their passion, enthusiasm and drive, which may have been dormant for several years. If, however, the exercise has the reverse effect (and this happens occasionally), you may have to reframe your client by pointing their focus away from past failures and towards their future successes now they have your help and support in helping them to take control of their own future.

One of the benefits of the life-story exercise, from your point of view, is that you get an instant overview of your client's history. This will help you to guide the client away from past behavioural traps and towards patterns of conduct that will support their goals and aims.

You can extend the life-story process by asking your client to transfer the major life-shaping events onto a line chart or graph illustrating their life in chronological order. The vertical axis can be marked 1 to 100, 100 being the highest point and 1 being the lowest point in your client's life. The horizontal axis should have the major events. Once your client has completed the chart it is easy for you to recognise the enabling or disabling repeating behavioural patterns or events. This information can be a valuable point of focus for accelerating changes in your client's behaviour and therefore changes in their results. If a client does not want to do the exercise, do not insist on completion: just work with what you already know. Remember that your client is the customer and, in this situation, the customer is right.

E-mail and Web Address

E-mail and a web address are becoming essential. They allow your clients to send you their goals and aims before your first coaching session. Encourage your clients to send you an e-mail at least 24 hours before each coaching call, with their current goal status. This gives you advance insight to the shape and direction of each call and uses the coaching time effectively. Clients adore this process because it holds them to their commitments and, by writing down their achievements, they become more tangible. Your clients gain the time to enjoy their own successes.

When funds permit, you should invest in a website and link it to as many of the big search engines as you can. Your site can even pay for itself in advertising revenue if you choose to organise contracts with suitable complementary but noncompeting companies.

Client Code-of-Conduct Document

A client code-of-conduct document, which covers the rules of conduct for clients, helps to put some structure around the coaching sessions and saves you constantly repeating what you expect from them. You can discuss any particular areas of the code of conduct on an individual basis if a client is uncomfortable with any aspect.

Here is an example of a client code-of-conduct document:

1. Always attend all meetings on time.
2. Always telephone at the agreed time.
3. Always be prepared for the coaching call:
    (a) Check what you have achieved against your tasks;
    (b) List what is still outstanding with your explanation for not completing the tasks and e-mail to me 24 hours prior to your next coaching session;
    (c) Consider what actions may be necessary prior to sessions.
4. Be honest at all times. Never lie about what you have achieved. It does not serve you.
5. You agree that I can challenge you if you are deceiving yourself or on any areas I see appropriate to do so.
6. Be willing and enthusiastic about trying new methods that I, as your coach, may suggest from time to time.
7. Accept and willingly work on direct, honest feedback received.
8. At all times work in partnership with me.
9. Be prepared to work on all areas of your life with me, not just your career. I am interested in your whole life not just a small part.
10. Arrange for payment to be made in advance of all coaching calls or meetings.
11. If you require a receipt request it in advance.
12. If you believe that you have received good service, please recommend life coaching to your friends.
13. Send any forms back promptly and fully completed.
14. Be prepared to step outside your comfort zone into an achievement zone with my support.

Please feel free to copy or adapt this code of conduct to send to your clients if you feel it will help to have a formal structure in place. It is an especially useful document when you first start to deal directly with your own paying clients, as it removes any potentially embarrassing moments.

The "Promise Document"

When I send out a client code of conduct, I usually enclose an "I promise to ..." document, which outlines my commitment to the client. This lessens any negative impact that the code might create. The "promise document" also helps you to focus on your outcomes, values, ethics and methods of working. Here is an example to give you the idea:

I promise, whenever possible:

1. to conduct all my dealings with you in absolute dignity, respect, honesty, confidentially, and as an equal;
2. always to conduct myself with integrity, responsibility and accountability;
3. always to attend all meetings on time;
4. always to answer the telephone at the agreed time;
5. always to be prepared for your coaching call;
6. to treat all information discussed with you or written to you with confidentiality: I will not divulge any part thereof to any third party, according to the Data Protection Act 1974/1998 amendments (excluding the police or a legal body);
7. to be committed to both the spirit and the letter of any agreements made with you;
8. always to ask in advance for written permission from you before releasing your name as referee;
9. not to defraud, misrepresent, deceive or mislead you;
10. to recommend the services of other institutions or professionals if appropriate to your outcomes; these services are offered without liability, obligation or redress to my company or myself;
11. to lift the bar just when you thought you had reached it;
12. to share with you all my knowledge, skills, experience and expertise where appropriate and when I deem necessary;

13. to challenge any self-deceptions that hinder your progress towards your ultimate outcomes;
14. to give you all the assistance, help, support, encouragement and guidance in fulfilling the outcomes or objectives agreed with me.

Sending out a document that clearly states your commitment will reassure nervous clients that your intentions are honourable and fair.

Safety

Working from your home can put your safety at risk, especially if you use printed marketing materials that include your home address. The safest way to avoid the risk is to use a PO Box number, which is easy to arrange with the post office within a few days. You simply complete a special form, send a cheque for the stated amount and send a recent original household bill (not a photocopy) to prove that you reside at the address you have given.

Using your home telephone number on printed marketing material can be another area for consideration as far as safety is concerned. Protect yourself from nuisance telephone calls by finding a telephone company that allocates an additional number that sits on top of your real telephone number. If you receive nuisance calls you simply cancel or change the top number. Another alternative is to purchase a lifetime number, which allows you to direct calls to different telephones. If you receive undesirable calls you can easily redirect them to the police or to your telephone line supply company who are trained to deal with problems of this nature.

By the very nature of life coaching, you sometimes deal with people at a very personal level and this can lead to complications. Clients can misconstrue a kind, sensitive gesture from a life coach as meaning that you want your relationship with them to be more intimate. Take great care to remain professional and emotionally distant when dealing with clients. A client's reaction may have nothing to do with your approach and everything to do with their inability to form proper relationships. You may become their target as a partner. This rarely happens with telephone clients but can happen with face-to-face coaching.

Always meet clients in public places or open-plan offices where people can see you, even if it is through a glass partition. This rule goes for male and female life coaches because, if you are completely alone with a client, you can become exposed to unfounded accusations. If you are female, never meet male clients in any place where you are alone with them or in a situation where other people are not within easy access. Meeting clients in busy five-star-hotel lounges gives a good upmarket impression and provides a degree of protection.

Ending the Contract or Coaching Programme

At the end of a coaching programme it is important to close the relationship well and to leave the door open for a future coaching relationship. Once you and your client have agreed to terminate the coaching sessions, always follow up with a thank-you card. Choose a card with an illustration of a subject close to the heart of your client. If your client owns a golden retriever dog, then send a card with a picture of a golden retriever! Do not send a picture of a poodle in the mistaken impression that all dogs are the same. Take your time and care to select a card that demonstrates your understanding of your client's likes and dislikes.

Write a simple thank-you along with a full reminder of the achievements made and the outcomes reached during your coaching sessions with this client. Express your gratitude for your client's confidence in your ability as a coach and for their patronage.

Mention that you are available for further coaching sessions when they need to achieve more goals. You can even offer them a one-off session price, which you will guarantee for the following twelve months or, perhaps, a special offer if they return to you within twelve months. Be as creative as you can with these offers. This gesture formalises the end of the coaching sessions, it leaves the client with a "feel-good factor" about your service, and it converts the service from one of "client service" to "client relationship," inviting a longer-term arrangement.

Referral System

On occasions, during client closure, I have included an offer that rewards the client for recommending others to my service. Take care that your client does not feel pressurised and that you do not cheapen your reputation. A most effective offer (measured in terms of response) has been "a further free coaching session for every recommendation provided." Please note that the offer is for the recommendation only and is not conditional on the referrals signing up for your service. This is important because, if you limit the offer to "clients gained," you may create friction and resentment from your exiting client. Remember that recommendations or referrals belong to your client and are their contacts. As an outsider relying on their goodwill, you must not abuse this privilege.

The last coaching call is as important as the first, because the future hangs on it. Clients purchase a programme of coaching sessions, usually at least four sessions but no more than twelve, with an option to renew on the final session.

It is perfectly ethical to encourage those clients who have achieved success in reaching the original outcomes to leave your practice if they have not indicated a desire to work on new objectives. Frequently, they do not wish to leave and request a further programme of coaching. If a spontaneous request is not forthcoming, you should remind them that this is the last session of the current series and ask if they would like to book another now.

When you are new to coaching and you are trying to build your practice, you may feel tempted to encourage your client to stay beyond the original contract, simply because you do not have any other clients waiting, you have bills to pay and you do need the money. Totally resist the temptation. If you yield, you will damage your relationship and they will be unlikely to help by giving you a list of referrals. More importantly, you will have put your own needs ahead of your client's interests and, when you do this, you have missed the whole point of life coaching.

A referral system will be your primary source of clients and should be treated with the utmost respect and care. Think of a time when you have been pressurised into purchasing something and then you resented the salesperson. In this case the salesperson is you and it will be you whom the client resents. An elegant way to encourage a continued partnership is to spend the final quarter of an hour reminding your client of the way that things were before the coaching started. Recall each achievement and, as you individually discuss it, ask your client to tell you how good they feel about each accomplishment. Then anchor this feeling (see Chapter Ten). When you have anchored all the good feelings ask, "You have [mention any outstanding goals]. You do still want to achieve them, don't you? So when now [set off anchor] will you book your next sessions to attain [the outstanding goals]?"

The outcome of this approach is that clients who really do not want to continue with further life coaching will immediately tell you so. Clients who are hesitant at this point will generally book further sessions. In my opinion, if clients are hesitant and they purchase further coaching because of the above approach, they truly do need more coaching. If a client rebooks after demonstrating hesitancy, I include a special coaching session dedicated to "how to make decisions with the feeling of absolute certainty."

It is well worth coaching your client in these skills because, at their next renewal time, they will be positive that they have made the best decision, whether they go or stay.

Training

Training as a life coach is important but not essential. Life-coach training is available, from a simple one-day event to full university accreditation. However, when you follow all the guiding principles in these pages, you need attend training courses only to network, to practise with other professionals or to receive accreditation. This book provides you with all the information that you require to coach clients and to grow your practice. Nevertheless, I do recommend that you join groups or organisations for professional life coaches.

There are groups of coaches who meet regularly to exchange professional information. There are electronic groups, chat rooms and other areas on the Internet where you can get advice, guidance and tips to improve your coaching style. You can participate by offering your experiences, advice and ideas.

Meeting with other coaches can offer you support, help in generating ideas, assistance for overcoming difficult client challenges and advice for improving your service to your clients. Life coaching can be a solitary profession with human contact restricted to your clients and social connections. Contact with other professionals is important, especially since your work can isolate you from the broader life coaching community.

Confidentiality

Always remember that client information is confidential and you must protect your client's identity at all times. If you are coaching a famous person there may be the temptation to show off by name-dropping. This is unacceptable and will eventually lead to loss of business, personal respect and your referral system. The identity of your clients should always be kept confidential unless your client agrees otherwise. Some clients will be proud to announce they have you as a their life coach. If such a client is willing for you to use them as part of your marketing campaign, ask for written "quotes" that you can use.

Matters of Administration

Bank Accounts

Bank accounts need to be arranged for the practice. The bank account has to be separate from your private account and all coaching income; both cheques and cash, should be put into this account. I recommend that you research the available banking services, as you can make big savings by selecting an Internet-based bank.

Your practice will not need the sophisticated services of a full-featured business account, as you will not generate huge quantities of individual transactions. Seek an account that offers the lowest charges for your particular situation. Some accounts that have higher charges for accepting deposits can still work out cheaper overall.

Value-Added Tax

Registration for value-added tax (VAT) is optional below a certain level of turnover and this level can be varied by the government at every budget time. You need to know the level at which registration becomes compulsory.

Some life coaches register for VAT before reaching the compulsory turnover level. This allows them to reclaim VAT on purchases for the practice. There are advantages and disadvantages to both choices. The only important thing is that you be registered when you need to be. As in all financial matters, you must seek the advice of a qualified professional.

Bookkeeping

Bookkeeping – your records of practice income and expenditure – must be kept up to date. Because a life coaching practice does not involve a lot of buying and selling, you could choose to keep your own books. If you want to take this route but lack the expertise, you could enrol on an appropriate course at your local technical college or buy a book that will explain the basics.

The alternative to keeping your own books up to date is to hire an accountant. The cost of this is tax-deductible, but do get a written estimate of your accountant's fees before you commit to anything. Fees and services vary enormously and it pays to shop around. Ensure total clarity on what you expect and what is expected from you, and seek personal recommendations from your own network of friends and colleagues.

Tax returns and National Insurance contributions are an unavoidable part of practice life, so do all that you can to keep good, simple records and stay within the law. Your accountant will be able to offer up-to-date advice on the latest situations as they affect your individual circumstances.

Data Protection

Data protection is an area that needs to be considered if, as you should, you are keeping records of your clients. You may not need to register within the rules of the Data Protection Act but you must check in relation to your circumstances, procedures and practice operation. Remember that ignorance of the law is not an acceptable defence argument.

Professional Indemnity

Professional indemnity insurance is highly recommended. As a profession, coaching is a benign process and it is virtually impossible to cause irreparable harm to a client. Alas, as litigation is seen by some warped individuals as a viable alternative to actually earning a living, you need to protect yourself against the risk of a threatened legal action, whether valid or opportunist. Again, the recommendation is to shop around and talk to other life coaches for the names of companies to contact – or to avoid.

And the Future?

Finally, I am an excellent coach but I am not a fortune-teller so I cannot predict the future of our profession. I believe that there will always be a need for coaching in one form or another and your coaching skills can be used anywhere in the world where you can speak the language. They are easily transferred to coaching within the workplace – where there appears to be an insatiable need for coaches. Some of my colleagues predict an exponential growth with saturation being reached only when *everyone* has a life coach. There are others who claim that life coaching is a new phenomenon with a short lifespan.

I do not know the answer. I do know, from my own experience, that life coaching improves all aspects of life for both the client and the coach. That seems a pretty good omen for a bright future.

Summary

- You must consider the market positioning of your service
- Marketing should take 40 per cent of your life coaching time
- Networking skills are essential
- Send out a client code of conduct
- Send a "promise" document
- Operate within the law
- Seek qualified professional advice for all financial matters

Chapter Nineteen

Specialist Life Coaching

*'The demand created the role and allowed a
holistic approach to include specialisation'*

Synopsis

**General life coaching and specialist life coaching are not mutu-
ally exclusive. In fact, they can be mutually inclusive. There are
several different specialisations but the most frequently consulted specialists are in relationships, wealth, health, spiritual
and career issues.**

**Relationship life coaches cover family, community, career and
general relationships. The wealth life coach needs to understand
what wealth is for each individual client. To excel as a health life
coach you must be an example of good health. The spiritual life
coach often links success and happiness with contribution, one
needing the other to produce the whole – whole being holistic.
The career life coach spends time on career planning and the
development of client skills to reach the career goals and the
planning of strategies necessary for career success.**

One of the rewarding aspects of life coaching is choosing to practise within one of the areas of specialisation. Once you have established a firm foundation and mastered the life coaching techniques
described in this book, then you can adapt them to suit an area of
expertise.

Life coaching is based on the concept that the coach should take a
holistic approach to a client's life and work on all areas simultaneously. This approach has been a catalyst to the founding of the profession, the demand for coaching services and the proliferation of
life coaches.

So, if a life coach encourages clients to balance their lives in all areas, it can appear to be a contradiction to introduce the notion of specialisation. And yet specialisation and a holistic approach are not mutually exclusive. On the contrary, they are mutually inclusive.

As the profession has developed it has attracted many diverse characters with a multitude of skills and knowledge. It is because of this, along with the fact that clients often present one or two areas in their lives with extensive deficits, that the specialist life coach came into being. The demand created the role.

Clients who believe they require assistance in only one area because they are content with the rest of their lives usually engage the services of a specialist life coach. This is not the only situation but it is generally the impetus for hiring a specialist. A coach with a general practice may refer a client to a specialist life coach if they feel that this will be in the client's best interests. There are many specialisations but the commonest include coaches who deal exclusively with issues such as relationships, wealth, health, spirituality and career progression.

Relationships

Relationship life coaches specialise in the areas of family, community, workplace and general relationships. Clients sometimes confuse this specialist coach with marital or personal organisations established for counselling. The significant differences are that the specialist coach will work with only one individual in total confidence – not with a couple. Also, a coach will examine the issues from the present and into the future, while a marriage-guidance counsellor will look to the past to see how the existing situation arose. Some life coaches are, in fact, trained and qualified counsellors, in which case they can deal with the case. Otherwise they would refer the client to a counsellor with the offer of ongoing coaching support. (See Chapter Three for an examination of the differences between coaching on the one hand and counselling and therapy on the other.)

However, relationship coaching has a far wider-reaching orbit than just marital matters. Humans are fundamentally creatures of community, and communities are based on relationships. The relationship life coach covers all aspects of relationship issues. During one coaching call they may be dealing with a manager–employee relationship and, during the next call, the issue could concern a personal friendship. It is this diversity of relationships that attracts coaches to this speciality. The core skills are the same as those of the general life coach. Both types of coach also share the belief that clients have all the resources and answers within themselves. This belief is essential for the relationship life coach, because they must remain dissociated from the emotion, from the heat of an issue and from the desire to offer advice.

You need two major strengths to specialise in relationship coaching. You must be able to keep yourself from becoming embroiled in the client scenario and thus risking the application of your model of the world to your client's current situation. It is a massive challenge for a life coach to sustain detached noninvolvement when a client is describing an emotional problem, particularly if the coach has experienced similar problems.

Emotional problems bring judgments. Some of these may be totally unfounded and unrealistically biased. For example, if a relationship life coach has suffered in the past from being subjected to wife battering and a client presents this problem, it is immensely difficult for that coach to remain nonjudgmental and emotionally dissociated. In this situation, the coach may start to make judgments and then to offer advice based on personal experience. Therefore, the second strength of the relationship life coach is the ability to refrain from offering advice throughout the coaching programme. If you cannot demonstrate the strengths of emotional dissociation and restraint from giving advice, then this specialisation is not for you.

Wealth

Wealth life coaching does not concentrate on the amount of income the client can generate, although this is a large part of the discussions. The wealth life coach initially needs to define the client's concept of wealth and the meaning that the word contains for that individual. Some clients will feel wealthy if they earn fifty thousand per annum. Other clients have a goal of a hundred thousand per annum. A few clients may even want a hundred thousand per annum from unearned income to free up time to spend with family and friends.

Every client has different goals and the wealth life coach will need to identify clearly the client's understanding of wealth. This specialisation will require a good understanding of client values and beliefs. A lot of time and effort can be wasted in coaching a client to reach their wealth goal – only to discover the client loses it all because of some erroneous belief pattern. For example, if a client believes that most rich people are crooks or that he or she is not worthy of owning riches, then as soon as they become rich they will be in conflict with a belief. The belief will eventually manifest itself either by the client's becoming a crook or losing the riches.

A financial background is not essential for a wealth life coach but it is helpful. However, good healthy beliefs about wealth generation and distribution are very important for a successful wealth life coach. One of the dangers for this specialisation is advice. Never give financial advice unless you are fully trained, registered and insured as an independent financial adviser. The only advice that a coach can offer is, "Seek an independent financial adviser." After this, you can coach on the goals agreed between the adviser and the client. An essential belief for every wealth life coach is that every client can be as wealthy as they want to be. Choose this specialisation only if you have this belief.

Health

There are many different aspects for a health life coach to concentrate on. For clients to become fully healthy they need a balanced diet and some form of exercise. The health life coach will work with the client in these areas. When you specialise in this area you must "walk your talk" and be a model of good health. You cannot be seriously overweight and eat junk food, especially if you are doing face-to-face life coaching. Incongruent beliefs and behaviours with this specialisation will eventually be revealed.

An understanding of nutrition or a background in physical education will be advantageous. If you have nutritional expertise, then you may develop a dietary plan with your client and suggest engaging the services of a personal sports coach for an exercise programme. Similarly, if you have sporting qualifications, you could recommend a nutritionist to your client. To excel as a health life coach you must be an example of good health yourself.

Spirituality

The spiritual life coach can be religious in the traditional sense – as in Christian, Jewish, Muslim, Buddhist or other recognised religion or denomination. The rules and beliefs of the particular religion of the coach will control the religious bias of the life coaching. The client base will probably be from the place of spiritual worship and both coach and client will share many of the same beliefs and values. The life coaching process will have strong guidelines and dogmas to follow and in some respects this will make the process easy to follow.

Spiritual life coaching can also take the form of guidance or contribution. This will depend on the individual spiritual life coach. Working as a specialist here requires total clarity about your boundaries. All spiritual life coaching needs to be marketed directly to the target audience. You must precisely describe the service on offer and take great care to avoid religious conflicts or implied attacks on profound matters of conscience. Be aware of the potential for spiritual misunderstandings, especially if these concern interpretation of esoteric concepts.

The contribution angle of spiritual life coaching is based in the belief that, in order to receive fulfilment, you need to give your time, expertise or finance. This form of life coaching focuses on how the client can contribute to the "greater good" in some way. Contribution of some form or other is seen as the pathway to total contentment. This spiritual life coaching develops a desire in the client to achieve absolute equilibrium between material, giving and sharing goals. The spiritual life coach links success and happiness with contribution, one needing the other to produce the whole – whole being both holistic and holy.

Career

Life coaching and specialist career coaching often go hand in hand. The career life coach spends time on career planning, development of skills to reach the career goals and the planning of strategies necessary for career success. To differentiate between a general life coach and a career life coach, we might say that they each adjust time allocations and the focus of their priorities.

In a typical life coaching session, time would be equally divided among all the areas of the life coaching matrix. There would be small variations in the time allocated for each session, but overall, throughout a typical period of twelve sessions, each of the matrix topics would have equal attention and time. Career life coaching would spend the largest amount of time on the career – up to 75 per cent, say – with a lesser amount on the other topics according to need.

A specialist career life coach would benefit from experience within the industry sector of the client, or a background in the career guidance field. This specialist coach could use career profiling or psychological assessment tests as an aid to the coaching programme. Of course, the career life coach could acquire these skills but it would be a great advantage if they were already in place.

If the career life coach has an industry background in common with the client, they will have insight to a number (the N of the I-CAN-DO model) of alternative ways of achieving client aims. Career life coaching can be very satisfying for both the coach and the client as progress takes place and the client achieves goals.

During the time that I specialised in career life coaching, one of my clients wanted to move from a middle-management position to become a director. After eliciting his goals and the current situation, I realised that he was task-focused and spent all his energy and time on achieving the stringent goals set for his department. There was no doubt that the goal would be achieved but he still felt the need to spend all his time and focus on ensuring the outcome. He believed that if he reached all of the target goals every year eventually he would be promoted. Here is a summary of the conversation we had:

COACH: What evidence do you have that achieving goals will give you the promotion you're looking for?

CLIENT: Well, it must. I always hit my targets!

COACH: How long has it taken in the past to get promoted?

CLIENT: About two to three years.

COACH: So, with that in mind, how long would it take for you to become a director?

CLIENT: Oh, I see what you mean. I would be retired before I got there.

COACH: Have you considered finding a mentor to help you?

CLIENT: No.

COACH: Who would be a good mentor for you?

CLIENT: Well, perhaps my boss's manager would be willing to help.

COACH: Is he or she a board member?

CLIENT: No, but I couldn't ask a board member.

COACH: What prevents you from asking a board member?

CLIENT: They are too busy to spend time with me.

COACH: Have you ever asked one of the board members before?

CLIENT: No.

COACH: How do you know they would be too busy to mentor you?

CLIENT: Well, I just know.

COACH: What's your commitment level on a scale of one to five – five being passionately committed – to becoming a member of the board?

CLIENT: Five.

COACH: Five?

CLIENT: Five.

COACH: What would happen if you asked your managing director if he would be your mentor?

CLIENT: He'd probably say no.

COACH: OK. Now let us say you contact your managing director and inform him of your goal to become a board member within two years. You admire the leadership qualities he has portrayed and you would like him to be your mentor. What are the most likely outcomes?

CLIENT: He says no.

COACH: He could also say yes, but I'll deal with that in a moment. So he says no. Could you ask him who on the board would he recommend you to ask to be your mentor?

CLIENT: Well, I suppose so.

COACH: So. Now you have a board member that the MD has rec-ommended. When you tell this board member that the MD has recommended him or her, what do you suppose they will say: yes or no?

CLIENT: Yes, I suppose

COACH: Correct. They are more likely to agree than disagree and you've now found a high-profile mentor? So you win. Now let's go back to the MD saying yes – this would also be a win, would it not?

CLIENT: Well, yes.

COACH: This sounds like a win-win for you?

CLIENT: Mm.

COACH: What day now would be a good time to approach the MD?

CLIENT: Well, I suppose I could ring his secretary as soon as I come off the call and arrange an appointment.

COACH: Will you?

CLIENT: Yes, I will do it now. I have nothing to lose and a mentor to gain.

My background in the industry gave me the edge when career life coaching with this client. Also, recognising a pattern of behaviour and its consequences within that industry enabled me to help my client "look above the parapet" and take a leap of faith. He is now a board member.

Summary

- Specialisation can offer very rewarding results for the coach
- Life coaching is founded on the idea that the coach should take a holistic approach to a client's life and work on all areas simultaneously
- The demand created the role
- Specialities include relationships, wealth, health, spiritual and career

Bibliography

Abraham, J., *Money-Making Secrets of Marketing Genius Jay Abraham and Other Marketing Wizards*. CA, USA: Abraham, 1993.

Beck, D.E. & Cowan, C.C., *Spiral Dynamics: Mastering Values, Leadership, and Change*. Oxford: Blackwell, 1996.

Berman-Fortgang, L., *Take Yourself to the Top*. London: Thorsons, 1999.

Cameron-Bandler, L., *Solutions: Enhancing Love, Sex, and Relationships*. Moab, USA: Real People Press, 1985.

Carlson, R., *Don't Sweat the Small Stuff at Work*. London: Hodder & Stoughton, 1999.

Charvet, S.R., *Words That Change Minds*. V.S.A., Iowa: Kendall/Hunt, 1994.

Covey, S., *Seven Habits of Highly Effective People*. London: Simon & Schuster, 1989.

Canfield, J. & Hansen, M.V., *A 2nd Helping of Chicken Soup for the Soul*. London: Vermilion, 1999.

Creffield, S., "The Spiral Staircase," *Rapport* no. 44, 1999.

Gallwey, T., *The Inner Game of Tennis*. London: Random House, 1975; Jonathan Cape, 1975.

Gallwey, T., *The Inner Game of Golf*. London: Random House, 1979; Jonathan Cape, 1981.

Harrold, F., *Be Your Own Life Coach*. London: Hodder & Stoughton, 2000.

Jeffers, S., *Feel the Fear and Do It Anyway*. London: Century, 1987.

McLaren, I.R., *Communication Excellence*. Carmarthen: Crown House Publishing, 2000.

Mehrabian, A., *Silent Messages: Implicit Communication of Emotions and Attitudes*. Belmont: Wadsworth, 1971.

O'Connor, J. & Prior, R., *Successful Selling with Neuro-Linguistic Programming*. London: Thorsons, 1995.

O'Connor, J. & Seymour, J., *Introducing Neuro-Linguistic Programming*. Wellingborough: Aquarian, 1990.

Richardson, C., *Take Time for Your Life*. London: Bantam, 2000.

Robbins, A., *Unlimited Power*. New York: Simon & Schuster, 1986.

Robbins, A., *Notes From a Friend*. New York: Simon & Schuster, 1991.

Semler, R., *Maverick*. London: Century, 1993.

Smith, R., *Up Your Aspirations*. Rugby: Pau, 1996.

Tolkien, J.R.R., *The Hobbit*. London: George Allen & Unwin, 1996.

Tracey, B., *Maximum Achievement*. New York: Simon & Schuster, 1993.

Whitmore, J., *Coaching For Performance*. London: Nicholas Brealey, 1992.

Other

Cainer, J., *Daily Express*, London, 21 August 2000.

Author Resource Guide

If you would like to contact Curly Martin you can do so through the publisher or directly at the following address. Curly welcomes discussions about all of the services mentioned below and is happy to answer any questions you may have.

Message from Curly (2005)

"I have received many requests for practical support, the opportunity to experience some of the coaching models, to see demonstrations, to take part in guided coaching practice and the chance to ask me direct questions. In response to these requests, I have designed the Life Coaching Handbook Diploma programme. If you would like to experience the passion and challenge of being coached by me or you would like to achieve the prestigious LCH Dip. qualification, please visit my website for details. I would love to meet you."

Curly Martin is the founder of:

Achievement Specialists

> **E-mail:** curly@achievementspecialists.co.uk
> **Websites:** www.achievementspecialists.co.uk
> www.curlymartin.com
> **Tel:** +44 (0)1264 326229
> **Free phone:** 0800 191 0200

Achievement Specialists offer the following courses:

> Life Coaching Handbook Diploma LCH Dip.
> The Corporate Coach

Services: Life Coaching, Business/Corporate/Celebrity Coaching

Author Profile

Curly Martin is the founder of Achievement Specialists Limited, a life coach training company; fellow of the European Coaching Institute; a qualified teacher (University of Sussex); and an internationally qualified master practitioner of Neuro-Linguistic Programming (NLP). A pioneer of life coaching in Europe, she was invited to join the Professional Speakers Association and is also a member of the Society of Authors. Curly is a highly successful and sought-after life, corporate and business coach. She intuitively combines accepted methodology with the cutting edge innovations of NLP to create an exciting, entertaining and effective approach to individual growth potential. In 1992 she was diagnosed with an aggressive form of cancer and given nine months to live. She used some of the techniques described in this book to alter the course of her life and she is passionate and inspirational about the transforming effects of life coaching. Gold medal achievers have coaches to support, encourage, motivate and raise the bar just when it has been reached. Curly believes every life has gold medal potential.

Index

The Life Coaching Handbook 2 Audiobook

Curly Martin with Janey Lee Grace

The
Life Coaching
Handbook

Everything You Need To Be An
Effective Life Coach

Curly Martin

Following the success of *The Life Coaching Handbook* Curly
Martin has recorded a 2 CD set to accompany the book,
narrated by BBC Radio 2's Janey Lee Grace.

CD 1
1. Introduction
2. Life Coaching Defined
3. Life Coaching Explained
4. Coaching versus
   Counselling and Therapy
5. Essential Coaching Beliefs
6. The Secrets of Coaching
   Success
7. How to Build Your
   Coaching Practice

CD 2
1. Introduction
2. The History and
   Development of Neuro-
   Linguistic Programming
   (NLP)
3. Essential Communication
   Skills
4. Fundamental Rapport Skills
5. Reframes
6. Matters of State
7. Representational Systems
8. Coaching for Results

ISBN: 9781904424697

www.crownhouse.co.uk
www.crownhousepublishing.com

The Business Coaching Handbook

Everything You Need To Be Your Own Business Coach

Curly Martin

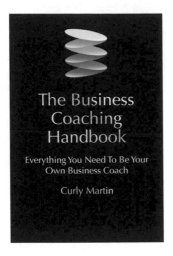

The Business Coaching Handbook reveals what business coaching IS, how to assess the shape of your business and what steps you need to put in place to grow it successfully.

Compiled for business entrepreneurs who have achieved the first goal of getting their enterprise up and running, or have been operating their own professional practice or business for a few years and now want to take it to the next level.

Set in a user-friendly format, *The Business Coaching Handbook* coaches the reader through a step-by-step process to business improvement. It is all about knowing where you are, where you are going and the actions that you need to take to get there.

ISBN: 9781845900601

www.crownhouse.co.uk
www.crownhousepublishing.com

The Personal Success Handbook
Everything You Need to be Successful

Curly Martin

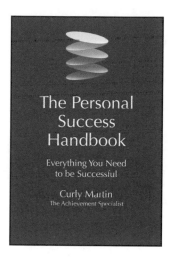

We are all different and success means different things to different people. Aimed at the individual, leads readers on a journey to define success. Once defined, Curly encourages us to look at ways to be successful in many different elements of life. Chapters include:

- health
- wealth
- happiness
- leadership
- entrepreneurship
- careers
- spirituality
- relationships
- emotions and many more

The Personal Success Handbook gives the reader the techniques, methodologies, tips, ideas, inspiration and practical guidance needed for success.

ISBN: 9781845900908

www.crownhouse.co.uk
www.crownhousepublishing.com